£1-50

CW00701376

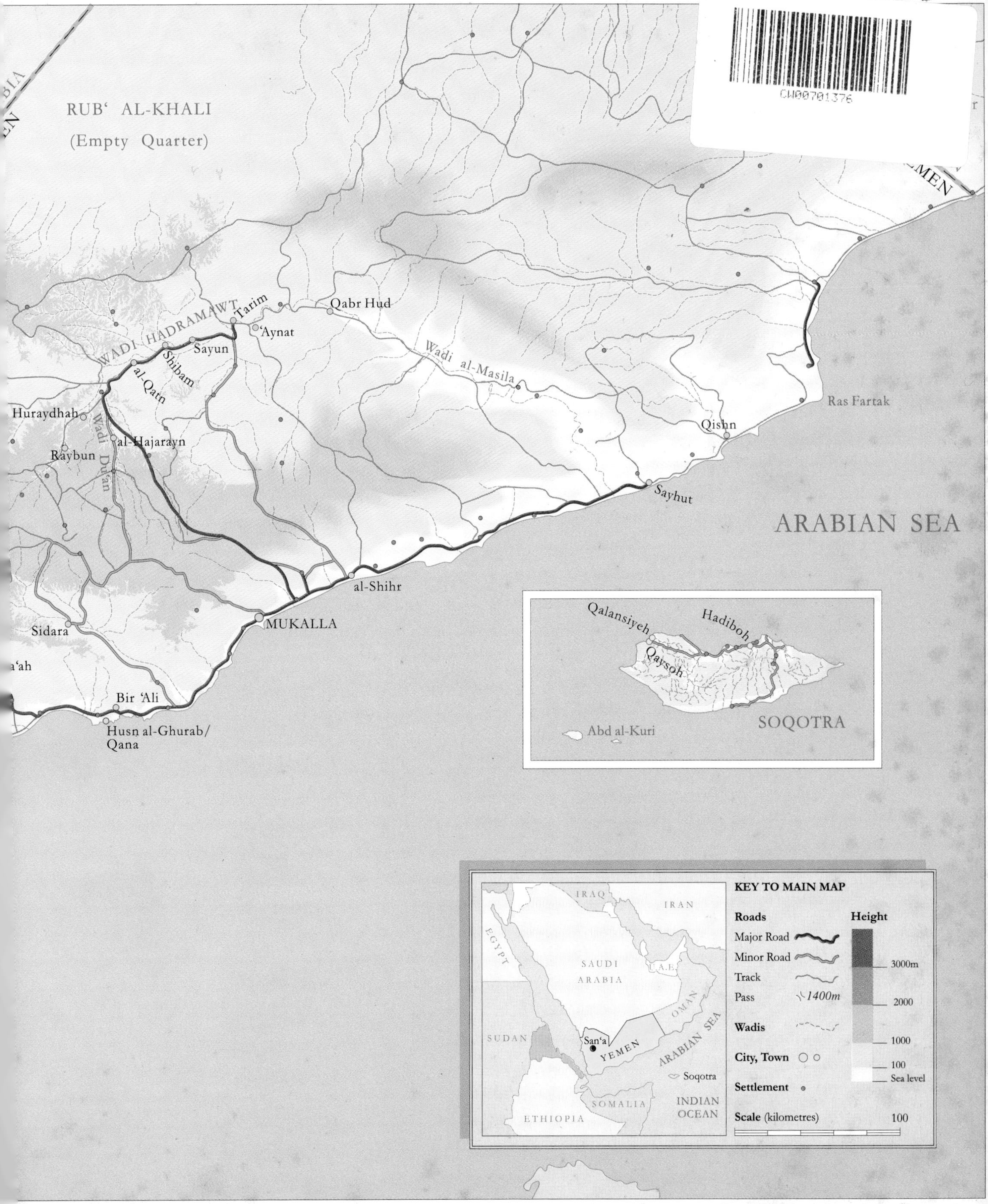

RUB' AL-KHALI
(Empty Quarter)

YEMEN

WADI HADRAMAWT

Tarim
Qabr Hud
'Aynat
Sayun
Shibam
al-Qatn
Wadi al-Masila
Huraydhah
Wadi Dulan
al-Hajarayn
Raybun
Ras Fartak
Qishn
Sayhut

ARABIAN SEA

al-Shihr

Sidara
MUKALLA

'ah

Bir 'Ali
Husn al-Ghurab/
Qana

Qalansiyeh
Hadiboh
Qaysoh

Abd al-Kuri
SOQOTRA

KEY TO MAIN MAP

IRAQ
IRAN
EGYPT
SAUDI
ARABIA
U.A.E.
SUDAN
OMAN
San'a
YEMEN
ARABIAN SEA
Soqotra
ETHIOPIA
SOMALIA
INDIAN
OCEAN

Roads	Height
Major Road	
Minor Road	3000m
Track	
Pass 1400m	2000
Wadis	1000
City, Town ○ ○	100
	Sea level
Settlement •	
Scale (kilometres)	100

Special thanks go to our sponsors,

Mr Dirham Abdo Saeed of Longulf Trading (UK) Limited

LONGULF

and the Hayel Saeed Group

Thabet Bros. Group & BP Middle East, Dubai

Christmas 004

to the adventurous Andersons~
whose heart is to travel to distant
places to explore.... and to serve.
enjoy!   with our love,
Gerry & Tessa

YEMEN
LAND AND PEOPLE

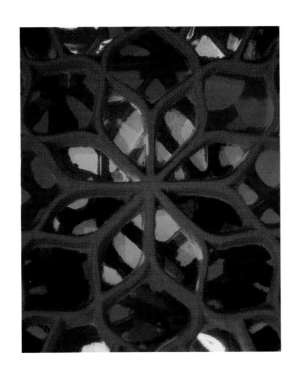

YEMEN

Land and People

TEXT BY
SARAH SEARIGHT

PHOTOGRAPHY BY
JANE TAYLOR

MIRANDA MORRIS
ON SOQOTRA

FOREWORD BY
TIM MACKINTOSH-SMITH

PALLAS ATHENE

Contents

Page 2: *A mudbrick tower house surrounded by farmland near Sayun, Wadi Hadhramawt*
Opposite: *The village of Hajarah above clouds that rise in the mornings from the hot Tihama plain into the Haraz mountains*

Acknowledgements

Sarah Searight: The Yemenis are a notably hospitable people, providing limitless cultural and physical sustenance for the researcher, the traveller and the inquisitive; and in their remarkable country I have had some of the most pleasurable and enriching experiences of my years around the Middle East. I would particularly like to thank Professor Dr Abdullah Abdulwali Nasher, chairman of the Yemeni-British Friendship Association, for his crucial encouragement and introductions; H.E. Dr Abu Bakr al-Qirbi, Foreign Minister; and H.E. Mr Abdul Wahab al-Rawhani, Minister of Culture; Professor Yusuf M. Abdullah, President of GOAM; H.E. Dr Husain al-'Amri, former Yemeni ambassador to the UK; Mr Ahmed Jaber Afif, founder of the al-Afif Cultural Foundation. I have frequently travelled under the well-organised auspices of Universal Travel; Marta Colburn, then of the American Institute of Yemeni Studies, allowed me the run of the Institute's excellent library; Mrs Frances Guy, British ambassador in Yemen, and Mr Adrian Chadwick of the British Council were also most helpful. Mr Abdul Wasa Hayel Saeed gave me some wonderful hospitality during a stay in Yemen, as did so many others – thanks to them all. A special debt of gratitude to Tim Mackintosh-Smith for providing a foreword – what better credential for a book about Yemen – and to a special friend, Dr Amina al-Nasiri, whose friendship opened so many Yemeni doors.

There are of course many aficionados of Yemen in Yemen and Britain to whom I nervously submitted my text. They include John Shipman and Francine Stone, Venetia Porter and Ken Kitchen and again Tim Mackintosh-Smith. They all know the subject far better than I do and I am extremely grateful to them for sparing the time to correct my errors. Enormous thanks go to the patient Ava Li for her editing of the text, and thanks also to my proof-reader Judith Eagle, whose observant eye corrected many a slip. Remaining errors are entirely my responsibility.

Above all I thank my husband Julian Lush who introduced me to Yemen in the first place and who has always been the most generous, patient and long-suffering of companions.

Jane Taylor: I set off to Yemen with huge ambitions as to what I hoped to see and photograph in that magical country, but lower expectations of what I might achieve. Abundant thanks are due to many people who contributed to realising most of my hopes, and easing the way for me and Isabelle Ruben, my excellent travelling companion. H.E. Mr Hassan al-Lowzi, then Yemeni Ambassador to Jordan, made all initial contacts, in particular an introduction to H.E. Mr Yahya al-Arashi, then Minister of Culture and Tourism. The Ministry, with the General Tourism Authority, generously provided hotel accommodation in San'a and elsewhere. Hamish Daniel, Deputy Head of Mission at the British Embassy in San'a gave me introductions to helpful individuals and companies. Peter Lindstrom, Tourism Director of SSI, with supreme generosity not only provided an excellent vehicle, but also the incomparable Mohammad al-Seif, who drove us safely and tirelessly, looked after us and made us laugh. Total Yemen, thanks to its General Manager Mohammad Zaki, allowed me to photograph from the company plane in Wadi Hadhramawt, while the Total prospecting team welcomed us at their nearby base camp. ABM Tours in San'a and a group of the German-Yemeni Friendship Society led by Dr Wolfgang Wranik allowed us to join their trip to Soqotra. Mr Abdul Wasa Hayel Saeed, of Hayel Saeed Anam & Co, arranged my visit to Hodeida. Arabian Horizons gave me a car, driver and guide (the excellent Ibrahim al-Kibsi) to get to Shaharah and Sa'dah. Dr Abdul Aziz al-Saqqaf, sadly deceased editor of the Yemen Times, and his wife Aziza, provided valuable information and much hospitality. Don and Raghda McLean, with quiet munificence, lent their house for the last week of my visit. And Ziad al-Rifai, a Jordanian friend then with UNICEF in San'a, never failed in his abundant generosity and humour, taking us on dawn visits to photograph in the early light, and providing frequent breakfasts, lunches, dinners and sanity. To all of you – and to all the warm-hearted Yemenis who made my time in their country so delightful and rewarding – my heartfelt thanks.

Opposite: *Fields and irrigation walls near Shabwah, Hadhramawt*

Foreword

by Tim Mackintosh-Smith

A few years ago, I rode to the top of the Mountain of the Prophet Shu'ayb on my motorcycle. It was hardly an achievement: in shape the mountain is more Ilkley Moor than Matterhorn. Even so, in the whole vast subcontinent of Arabia there was no human as high; or only Shu'ayb, lying in his tomb-chamber by the summit. Beneath me the earth fell away in a jumble of broken arcs and planes. The solitude was dizzying.

And yet, this being Yemen, I was not alone even at 12,000 feet. Through the rush of wind I could just hear other sounds, coming from the tomb – the rhythmic sound of sweeping, then a woman's voice. Minutes later I was sharing lunch with a tribesman from al-Haymah. With his wife and children, he had walked since dawn to visit the prophet and give him a spring clean. They were clearly not well off – lunch was dry barley bread and water – and when the inevitable stream of questions came to the matter of my salary, I was relieved to be able to reply in all honesty that I had none. The Haymi looked aghast, stuck his hand in his pocket and offered me a fistful of banknotes.

The money was returned to the pocket, but only after the use of physical force on my side. We parted with blessings, and I began my bowel-loosening descent.

It was not an everyday meeting, but it was quintessentially Yemeni in its features. There are the human ones – generosity, piety, tenacity, inquisitiveness (one sometimes feels interrogated; one never feels ignored). And there is the setting, this great glittering wrinkled country of peaks and plains, towers and surprises, in which unexpected encounters in out-of-the-way spots are, paradoxically, almost predictable. You will try to get away from it all in vain: people are ubiquitous, the land itself possessive. 'Not a day will pass in your life,' wrote the Master of Belhaven, who had soldiered and wandered in the contorted interior of the old Aden Protectorate, 'but you will remember some facet of that opal-land; not a night will pass without some twist of dream.'

How to put it all across? Yemen is almost indecently well endowed. While it missed out on the languid studio-orientalism of the nineteenth century, in the twentieth it became the cynosure of travelling lenses – those of Hans Helfritz, Daniel van der Meulen and Pascal Maréchaux among them. Jane Taylor belongs to a tradition of lady photographers in Yemen that goes back over a century, via Freya Stark to the remarkable Mrs Theodore Bent. This latter and unsung heroine coped with the considerable impedimenta of a Victorian travelling darkroom in the unlikeliest spots, from the palmeries of Hadhramawt to secluded dells on the island of Soqotra. (I envy her most her description of a tribal shaykh in the Wadi Bin Ali as 'a very elastic and naked sovereign'.)

Opposite: *Luhayyah; gaily painted fishing boats at anchor*

Yemen is inexhaustibly photogenic. An American photographer, jaded by a surfeit of supermodels, told me that in it he had at last found the Holy Grail of photography. But Yemen is also the victim of its own photo-genius. The alluring images of veils and daggers, guns and qat, dished out *ad nauseam*, have become the ocular equivalent of fast food. Gobbled up by picture editors and regurgitated in the press, they tend to nourish a conception of the place as introverted, indolent and threatening. The pictorial clichés are certainly here; but many of the inferences drawn from them by journalists on two-day sprees bear about as much relation to the real Yemen as Disney's Aladdin does to the real Baghdad. Part of the importance of a book like this is to show that the visual feast is of far greater subtlety and complexity.

Sarah Searight's text is an elegant excursion around the most topographically diverse part of the Arab world and the fountain-head of its culture. Early on she puts her finger on a characteristic of Yemen: the individualism of its people. It is perhaps the surest thread to follow through the Daedalian twists of the country's history. Other visitors have remarked it. Seventy years ago, for instance, the Syrian traveller Nazih al-Azm wrote: 'The Yemenis are, to a man, free in their convictions and independent in their opinions. They do not abide injustice, neither will they bow to indignity or servility.'

Like the fly of prophetic tradition that contains infection in one wing and cure in the other, this irrepressible independence is Yemen's bane and its balm. It creates tensions between state control and tribal freedoms, and yet it has seen off the British and the Ottomans (a Turkish commander of the nineteenth century said that with a thousand men of al-Haymah – forebears of my host on the mountain – he could take the whole of Europe). It does not suffer authority gladly; but it has also never suffered authoritarianism, and it never will.

Predictions – apart from that last phrase – are probably pointless. But perhaps the fourteenth-century Egyptian writer al-Umari got it right: 'If Yemen were to be united under one ruler, its importance would increase and its position among the eminent nations would be strengthened.' The two former states of Yemen were unified in 1990. More recently the country has solved its longstanding border dispute with Saudi Arabia. Its population is the most numerous and the most energetic in the Arabian Peninsula. Its economy is stabilising, and in Aden it has the finest port in the Indian ocean. Yemen's future may well be as glittering as its landscape, and as full of surprises.

Tim Mackintosh-Smith,
Bayt Qadi, San'a,
Yemen

To the reader

The aim of this account of Yemen is to introduce newcomers succinctly to the history and scenery of this remarkable country, and to encourage them to read further, using the select bibliography and the endnotes, which give details of some of the many books and articles on Yemen. As always, geography dictates history, and so our chapters have somewhat geographical headings, but they do also follow a kind of chronology, which is summarised and clarified at the end in a chronology of main events. A glossary is also included for Arabic terms used in the text. Italics are used only the first time an Arabic word is used. Transliteration of Arabic is always a nightmare but I have tried to be as accurate as one can be without using diacriticals, except for ', which is used for the Arabic guttural consonant, 'ayn.

Sarah Searight

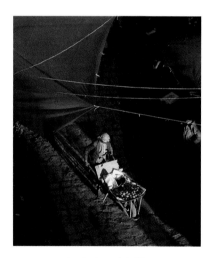

San'a: Suq al-Milh

I 'A COUNTRY FAIR IN ITS WATER AND AIR'

So the Syrian-American traveller Ameen Rihani was assured in 1922 by a Yemeni companion.[1] First impressions of Yemen are more dramatic; the landscape erupts through the early morning mist like the dawn of creation, the geological upheavals of this corner of Arabia inscribed on its escarpments, in its gorges, over its lava-strewn plateaux. Yemenis tell the story of how God decided to visit the world he had created. He went first to London – 'changed a lot,' he said, 'since I made the place.' Then he went to Egypt – 'quite different,' he said, 'from what I created.' Finally he came to Yemen. 'Ah, that I recognise!' He said. 'That hasn't changed since the day I created it.' The narrators have a point but they ignore man's sculpting of the western escarpment over thousands of years, a densely woven tapestry of terraces draped down the precipitous mountainside.

The Yemeni mountains belong geologically to Africa – vast outpourings from the intense volcanic period that occurred four hundred and fifty million years ago. Around ten million years ago the Rift Valley began to be formed, a process of splitting and lifting landmasses that separated Asia from Africa, Yemen from the Horn of Africa, and formed the mountains of Ethiopia and Yemen.[2] The process is still happening; the formation of the Red Sea, with its crucial opening to the Indian Ocean at the Bab al-Mandab, is part of the continuing movement of the Afro-Asian plates along the Rift Valley fault, demonstrated in regular tremors and the occasional quake. No recent volcanic eruptions have occurred on land, however; the last is thought to have happened at least a thousand years ago.[3] But all the variety and colour of rocks raised by giant tectonic movement will be seen caught in the building materials used everywhere by Yemenis with the strong decorative sense one soon learns to associate with them.[4]

Those Rift Valley movements, the upward tilt of western Arabia, explain the country's geography. They created, for instance, the country's hot, humid coastal plain, called Tihamah, which emerged from the Red Sea in geologically recent times. Some 25–50 kilometres wide, the coastal plain is halted by a near-vertical escarpment that parallels the Red Sea. At its foot is a succession of hot springs – another demonstration of that geological ferment. The springs, fed into smelly cavernous pools, are almost too hot to enter; in one of them, 'Ayn al-Sukhna, the last Imam but one used to soak his ailing, ulcerated body.

Few roads lead up and over the escarpment. In the late nineteenth century the Ottoman Turks then governing Yemen invited the French to build a railway connecting the port of Hodeida with their headquarters in San'a; the track struggled a few

Opposite: *Patches of green in the southern highlands; agricultural terraces utilise every square inch of fertile soil*

miles out of town but sensibly gave up before turning vertical. The Cold War eased the problem of communication, with rival powers competing to bring the blessings of modern engineering in the form of what roads there are. But much of the time one climbs up and down skilfully laid basalt stairways that connect villages clustering on rocky outcrops like shipwrecked sailors, leaving any space that is not completely vertical to be banked into terraces for coffee (on the lower slopes), grain and the ubiquitous and mildly stimulating *qat*, a plant chewed by Yemenis most afternoons. Women still walk up and down the stairways with vats of clean water from springs that may be several hours' walk from home, bedecked with lumps of coral and turquoise and silver beaten from Maria Theresa thalers, the old currency of Arabia.

From the top of the escarpment, crowned by Arabia's highest mountain, Jabal al-Nabi Shu'ayb at 3,700 metres, one descends slightly to the highland plains, undulating from north to south, dotted with diminutive volcanic cones like childrens' sand-castles; the fields between the lava flows are green in the growing season with sorghum and wheat, vines and qat, watered by expertly engineered irrigation channels, all too often nowadays augmented by the diesel pump. To the south, beyond the dramatic Sumarah Pass, are the greenest areas of Yemen, well watered by monsoon rains. The highlands slope upwards to the east to the Sarat mountain chain, and then down to the dry flat lands that ring the great Arabian desert, the sands of Ramlat Sab'atayn (known also as the Sayhad) leading to the so-called Empty Quarter or Rub' al-Khali. Out here

Dunes in the Rub' al-Khali

Cistern in the town of Hababa. Rainwater is collected for pre-prayer ablutions at the mosque at the further end, before being released into the cistern and thence to gardens and fields below the town

in the east is one of Yemen's oilfields. Mountain wadis debouch towards the desert; in the past they watered the ancient kingdoms of the desert fringe before losing themselves in the sands of the Empty Quarter. These prosperous settlements of ancient Arabia, the Sayhadic kingdoms, flourished from at least the first millennium BC, their prosperity initially due to the collection and diversion of water from the highlands to agriculture; this in due course accounted for the other cause of their prosperity, provision of food and water to, and taxation of, the camel caravans travelling along the land trade route carrying spices from India, frank-

incense from what is now Oman, and myrrh. No wonder that the Romans named this corner of Arabia 'Arabia Felix'.

The most visibly volcanic landscape is in southern Yemen – 'a land of bitter-sweet contrasts,' wrote the Master of Belhaven in the 1930s.[5] Vast lava fields and cruel mountain ranges effectively obstruct communication, isolating tribal communities condemned until recently to perpetual rivalry for meagre resources. Aden itself, one of the finest harbours in the world, is situated on the rim of a volcanic crater, part of that same geological turmoil that also underlies the creation of the island of

Soqotra, some five hundred kilometres offshore.

Rain has been the essence of Yemeni civilisation, blown on to the escarpment and to a lesser extent the southern highlands by the south-west monsoon. It comes in small quantities in April and May, more heavily in July and August. 'A strange thing about the rain in India, Yemen and Abyssinia [Ethiopia],' complained the great fourteenth-century Tangerine traveller Ibn Battuta, 'is that it falls only in the hot weather and mostly in the afternoon [so] the townsfolk retire indoors for their rains are heavy downpours'.[6] They certainly can be; a wadi in spate may carry death and destruction as well as fertility. Lieutenant Cruttenden in 1836 learned that there had been no rain for three years but the flash flood that he met drowned his donkey and nearly swept him away. Even so, there is not a lot of rain; in fact relative drought is now a major problem for the burgeoning 18 million Yemenis (population growth, at 3.7 per cent, is one of the highest in the world). And the quantity of rain varies: in the 1970s Yemen was afflicted by the same drought as sub-Saharan Africa. Special prayers for rain are heard in the mosques most summers and there are still remnants of a ritual ibex hunt in Hadhramawt to ensure rain – sure signs of a precarious supply.[7]

But the little that falls is well used. It explains

Small lake in a volcanic crater at Damt, a popular hot spring resort for Yemenis

Wadi Rima, Tihama; women at work in the fields

the lushness of the well-watered highlands south of the Sumarah Pass (traditionally regarded as the dividing line between north and south), where the rainfall is around 800 millimetres a year, compared with the dryer north where it is no more than 400 millimetres. All over the country one comes across finely engineered water works: on that desert fringe the stately remains of the ancient Marib dam, the grandest engineering feat of antiquity, harnessing water from a vast collecting area; in the central highlands the extraordinary feat of a tunnel through a mountain at Baynun to carry water from the catchment area to fields the other side; in Aden a series of 'tanks' or cisterns spilling down the mountainside. Certain major wadis in the south can become torrents in the rainy season – Wadi Bana, for instance, a major route for people and goods between north and south (where its waters debouch to fertilise the rich Abyan plain) is impassable when in spate. Perhaps the most celebrated wadi is the Wadi Hadhramawt, which harvests a pitiably small rainfall from the surrounding plateau. When that failed Hadhramawt sent its population far and wide across the Indian Ocean. Agriculture in Tihamah is watered by wadi spate, generally well controlled as it falls down the escarpment and carefully diverted into fields of grain and cotton.

These are the dramatic examples; one comes across the less dramatic in every field, on every terrace, in every village. A village such as Hababa (see p. 18), perched fortress-like on a crag will direct rainfall to the mosque for ritual ablutions (obligatory before prayers); from there the water falls into the village cistern and is used for household purposes as well as by small boys diving in and out of its murk; and from there it is directed to the vegetable gardens on the edge of the village. You may quibble at the hygiene but never at the ingenuity.

Yemen is bordered to the north by Saudi Arabia, and by Oman to the east. (Relations with the latter are now cordial but were embittered in the 1970s by the support of what was then the People's Democratic Republic of Yemen – PDRY – for the rebellion in Dhofar). But equally significant is Yemen's relationship with the surrounding ocean – the Red Sea in the west, the Indian Ocean south and east. These have made Yemen the entrepôt between the Mediterranean on the one hand, and India and China on the other. The relationship is visible in its coastal people: those of Tihamah are strongly influenced by the proximity with Somalia and Ethiopia in face, dress, architecture and customs; those of Aden reflect the Indian connection; those in Wadi Hadhramawt illustrate the Far Eastern connection. Only in the central highlands and on the desert fringe does one find a more Arabian physiognomy – small, lithe, sharp-featured.

The main towns of Yemen are Sa'dah in the north, San'a the capital in the centre, Ta'izz and

Opposite: Hajarah in the Haraz mountains; the old Jewish quarter is at the foot of the hill

Chewing qat, *a regular afternoon occupation for most Yemeni men and an increasing number of women*

Aden in the south, Hodeida in Tihamah. But the majority of the population is still based in the countryside and dependant on agriculture. Sorghum, wheat and maize are the main food crops; the Yemenis are said to bake over a hundred different kinds of bread from these grains, the variety reflecting the country's wide-ranging contacts with the outside world. Lentils and fenugreek are other major crops. Thirsty lucerne is grown for domestic livestock. Coffee is grown in wadi bottoms and the lower slopes of the escarpment; the Yemenis prefer to drink an infusion of the husks flavoured with ginger and sugar known as *qishr*. But coffee and other food crops have in many areas been overtaken *qat,* less demanding and more in demand .

The tatty bushes of *Catha edulis* (so named by the first European botanist to visit Yemen, Peter Forskål, in 1763) or qat, the local name, occupy much of the agricultural landscape; some say it is the most important cash crop in Yemen. It is easily grown, requiring relatively little attention and not too much water. The leaves are harvested daily, taken to the nearest market, sold and consumed after lunch the same day. Yemeni men, and increasingly women, sit for two or three hours most days, masticating the leaves to shreds that accumulate in the cheek like a golf ball, and sucking on the juice that provides the mild stimulant. Yemenis extol qat; foreigners have tended to decry it. 'Most debilitating,' 'a poisonous drug,' 'widespread evil,' are some foreign comments. But a sixteenth century poet in Ta'izz praised it most eloquently: 'It illuminates the heart and frees the chest of sadness. It becomes the comrade of happiness: do not say it is bitter if you cannot have it, as did the fox of the grapes that did not fall into his jaws.' But really to appreciate its hold one should read a modern eulogy by a true devotee, Tim Mackintosh-Smith, in his *Yemen: Travels in Dictionary Land*, extolling the mood of reflection, contemplation which it induces, 'the still point of the turning world.'[8]

If the country itself is 'fair in its water and its air', what of the people who live there? These geologically and geographically diverse regions produce a diverse population – a mixture of Arabian, African, Indian, fiercely independent, proud of tribal affiliations, of the genealogy which gives them such a sense of historical continuity. For the newcomer the continuity is sustained in a sense of the ancient endeavours that mark the landscape – villages, castles, waterworks, generation after generation building with stones hewn by their ancestors. Names of ancient peoples are often preserved in place and tribal names.

But it is not easy to generalise about the

Yemenis; they have a strong streak of individualism. Two features in particular come to mind.
One is their liveliness. You see it in the way the
highlanders walk ('the swift hip-swing of the hills,'
as Belhaven put it[9]), often in shoes that seem too
big, a sort of swift lope that carries them up and
down cliffs, over plateau and desert. You hear it in
their conversation, often shouted across a valley,
summoning sleepy children to school, spreading
news of life and death. More subtly it is demonstrated in the long tradition of their music and
dance and poetry. More politically it is shown in
the fluctuating loyalties of tribal politics.

The other remarkable characteristic is the
Yemenis' decorative sense. At its most basic, men,
women and children love dressing up; they have
an astonishing variety of clothing – caps, shawls,

Below: *Girls in festival finery in San'a*
Right: *An elderly citizen of Jiblah, dressed up for
Friday prayers at the Great Mosque*

23

magnificent jewellery, kilt-like skirts, all worn with a panache that would be the envy of a Paris model. Less basic but no less visible is the decoration of their buildings. Sometimes this is in the decorative as well as structural use of the different rocks thrown up in repeated primordial upheavals (there are said to be forty-seven different colours). In stone architecture the ubiquitous tufa is sandwiched between purple-black basalt and purple-red granite; mud and mud-brick buildings are ringed with painted designs, the colours of which are ground from local minerals.[10] Mosques are covered with carved stucco decoration, their ceilings with swirling abstract designs. There's a stylish fantasy about those urban palaces of Hadhramawt, the tower houses of Shibam; a walk at night through the streets of old San'a, the coloured glass in the windows lit up from within, will demonstrate this sense of colour and style.

In the market of San'a, the main street of Ta'izz, the back alleys of Aden's Crater, the stranger is immediately entangled in a mélange of cultures that is as uniquely Yemeni as the piping hot meat stew, *saltah*, spiced with flavours from Africa and India as well as Yemen itself. Many Yemenis eat saltah for lunch before settling down for an

Basalt is used in this house façade to highlight architectural features and add a contemporary contrast to the dominant tufa stone

afternoon's 'chew'. Yemeni cuisine has a limited range but is far more varied than any other on the Arabian peninsula; a delicious bowl of saltah in all sorts of ways typifies the country's position astride major trade and pilgrimage routes.

The very name 'Yemen' has been used for this corner of Arabia since at least at least 300 AD, and as one moves around the country one discovers the sense of continuity that permeates Yemeni society: environment, tradition (enshrined in interminable genealogies) and religion have moulded it for thousands of years and still do – dominating the lives of those who live there, their architecture, their decorative traditions, their rich and enduring literature, their relationships.

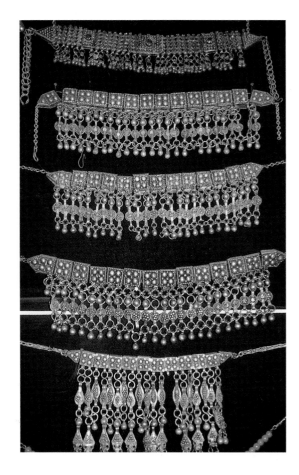

Silver jewellery on display in San'a. Much of this used to be made by Jewish craftsmen

25

II THE ANCIENT KINGDOMS IN THE EAST

In July 1843 Thomas Arnaud, a French pharmacist who had been working for the Ottomans, set off for the small town of Marib on the edge of the desert, site of ancient temples and dam and known source of inscriptions in an undeciphered but elegantly formed script. The journey took six days and tribal suspicions restricted his visit to two days but in between confrontations with the locals (anyone digging holes in their territory must surely be looking for gold) he managed to find and copy fifty-six of the finely carved inscriptions of a South Arabian language. Another Frenchman Joseph Halévy made his way to Yemen in 1869–70 and returned home with seven hundred inscriptions. In the 1880s Edouard Glaser, fascinated by these earlier discoveries, visited Yemen four times, travelling much more widely than his European predecessors and subsequently publishing extensive archaeological, philological, ethnographic and geographical notes on the country.[11]

These early explorers were revealing a civilisation that seemed to have emerged fully fledged in the first millennium BC and immediately linked by biblical scholars to the alleged visit of the Queen of Sheba to King Solomon described in I Kings (Solomon ruled during the tenth century BC). But the origins and development of that civilisation, what went before, remained a mystery that is now being slowly solved. The excavation of ancient sites was eased by the ending of the civil war in 1970 and a Department of Antiquities was established in northern Yemen (one already existed in the south);[12] unification between north and south in 1990 has also helped. Today archaeologists are less likely to be regarded as treasure seekers.

There are inevitably many question marks over

Opposite: *Marib: The Sabaean temple known as 'Arsh Bilqis, dating from at least the 1st millennium* BC

Right: *Minaean inscription from Baraqish, found near the temple of Nakrah*

27

the earliest human records in Yemen, and answers can still only be deduced by using parallels elsewhere in Arabia or the wider Middle East and East Africa. Assuming that *homo habilis* left Africa some two million years go, that still leaves an enormous gap to be filled before the first signs of Upper Palaeolithic man and his crude stone tools appear in escarpments of what was then a well-watered Hadhramawt around 700,000 years ago.[13] Russian, French and American missions have found traces of human occupation between then and the Neolithic period of around 8,000 years ago. The scene is complicated by evidence of climatic change, with alternating wet and dry periods; it is hard to imagine when one is in the midst of the arid gravel plain and dunes of Ramlat Sab'atayn but in one wet period alone the Wadi Jawf in the north-west may have been linked with Wadi Hadhramawt in the south-east, judging by evidence from a fossil lake near the desert fort of al-'Abr.[14]

In the Neolithic period man begins to make a more distinctive mark on the landscape. On the highland plateau east of San'a, in the area of Khawlan al-Tiyal, and east of Sa'dah in the north, Italians have found both Palaeolithic and Neolithic sites, the latter dating from around 6,000 BC.[15] The more sophisticated stone tools of Neolithic man enabled him to construct simple round huts, to develop rudimentary food crops, such as sorghum (with seed originally from east Africa) and wheat, and to practise animal husbandry. Rock art in the Sa'dah area, focusing on human figures and ibex, may mark the emergence of religious beliefs towards the end of the Neolithic period, around 4,000 BC.

There still remains a tantalising gap between the Neolithic and the emergence of sophisticated, urbanised South Arabian civilisation in the first millennium BC. Much research has been concentrated again on the slopes of Hadhramawt escarpments as well as on the surrounding plateau, the *jawl*, where soil erosion has led to the discovery of remarkable funerary monuments, including a series known elsewhere in Arabia that is distinguished by a 'tail' sometimes stretching several hundred metres. They are dated to the fourth to third millennia BC.[16]

Climatic change and desertification herald the Bronze Age of the third to second millennia BC.[17] Bigger communities were needed to organise complex irrigation systems, the traces of which are beginning now to be revealed in Hadhramawt and further west in Bayhan. They date back to the mid-third millennium, and are associated with more 'tail' tombs found by French archaeologists. In the Khawlan al-Tiyal area tombs, houses, some kind of communal religious building and pottery sherds also may be evidence of life in this Bronze Age. A small 25-centimetre piece of granite from the highlands, now in the National Museum, is carved in the simple phallic shape of an idol, testifies to early religious culture, but it is difficult to be more precise about this period; too few artefacts have been found to allow for more precise dating and vast areas of the country remain to be explored, including much of coastal Tihamah. But it seems likely that on the basis of existing discoveries there were already links with greater Arabia, even with the Persian Gulf and Mesopotamia, links that would be dramatically strengthened in the first millennium BC when South Arabian civilisation emerged.

Arnaud, Halévy and above all Glaser cast a brilliant light on South Arabia, whose early civilization is traditionally linked with the arrival in the south-west of Semitic-speaking tribes from the north. These tribes overwhelmed the more

*Aerial view of the old city of Marib,
which occupies a tell that may
contain the remains of the
pre-Islamic city.
Ancient stones are incorporated in
many of the houses as well as in
the small mosque on the middle
right of the picture*

primitive indigenous peoples, possibly of Kushite origin, similar to the peoples of the Horn of Africa. But the idea of primitive indigenous yielding to superior invading culture now seems misleading. Interesting pre-invasion settlements, probably Bronze Age, are being found in the mountain ranges west of Marib for instance, though local circumstances have prevented full excavation; and recent excavations at Sabr in the hinterland of Aden provide evidence of possible links not so much with the rest of Arabia but instead with Ethiopia and Eritrea, even Nubia and eastern Sudan. (Archaeology in the first two, however, is no more developed than in Yemen.) Unusual and highly skilful pottery, well-moulded figurines and the use of incense in Saba, are arguably part of a southern Red Sea civilisation pre-dating the arrival of the Semites from the north.[18]

29

A 1st century AD tablet, inscribed in the Sabaean script by one Lahay 'Athat dhu Nasam with a dedication to the sun goddess Shams, headed by a sun and moon motif. The crescent moon, also representing bull horns, was later adopted as the symbol of Islam. National Museum, San'a

The incursions of these Semitic tribes seem to have begun around the late second millennium BC. Among them were the Sabaeans, the Minaeans, the Qatabanians and the Hadhramis, tribal names given them by the third century BC Greek geographer Eratosthenes, later quoted by Strabo. They would have found settlements with irrigation works, and agriculture; and would have incorporated these technologies with their own to lay the basis of what became the highly developed civilisation of the ancient kingdoms of southern Arabia. These became known as the Sayhadic kingdoms, from the name given to the group of languages clustering on the edge of the sand desert of Ramlat Sab'atayn, al-Sayhad. The languages were distinct from each other, but the script, deriving from the Phoenician alphabet, was less so: Arab writers call it *musnad*, and it has affinities with scripts found in northern and central Arabia as well as with modern Ethiopian script. Decipherment was well under way by the end of the nineteenth century. Sabaean proved the easiest because it is closest to Arabic; Minaean and Qatabanian were more problematic because there are fewer inscriptions. The tribes are remembered today because of their role in the land-based aromatics trade, but it was their mastery of irrigation technology, and the agriculture they developed to finance the temples and palaces being excavated today, that drew the trade in their direction – that, and the domestication of the camel in the second millennium BC and its adaptation to the long-distance carriage of goods.[19]

The broader chronology of these civilisations is now more or less established, although there are no recorded dates in inscriptions until the second century AD.[20] Saba (Sheba) is the earliest 'state' of the four to be mentioned (in fact it was more of a tribal federation), in the Old Testament description of the legendary Queen of Sheba's visit to Solomon in the tenth century BC. There is no mention of such a queen in the Sabaean ruler lists and no reason to think one ever existed (she has also been claimed by the Ethiopians and most recently by the Nigerians; and as Bilqis she is claimed by the Arab world), but the biblical story does indicate established trade relations. In the eighth century BC a Sabaean ruler is recorded as bringing tribute to the Assyrian ruler Sargon II.

The two main centres of Sabaean civilisation were Sirwah and Marib. 'Mistress of cities,' wrote Pliny the Elder of Marib, 'the diadem on the brow of the universe.'[21] But virtually no secular buildings have yet been excavated to support his eulogy, perhaps because they are buried beneath the houses of what is known today as Old Marib; certainly plenty of inscribed stones are embedded in the walls of its houses, half ruined by bombing in the 1960s civil war. Inscriptions have identified a succession of rulers, initially a series known as *mukarrib*, replaced around 650 BC by straightforward secular kings. These rulers were responsible for government, the economy and construction; they built cities, temples, including two major shrines excavated at Marib, and dams.[22]

The great dam at Marib, whose present remains are such a striking reminder of the engineering skills of the Sabaeans, was the successor to many earlier structures. Eighteen metres high and earth-filled, it stretched 680 metres across the Wadi Dhana, marked now by great mounds of silt but designed to divert waters from a catchment area of some 10,000 square kilometres into fields on either side. The dam was intended to reduce the force of the flood and enable the water to pass through two sluices – North and South – on opposite banks of the wadi. The sluices were built of immaculately dressed masonry, clamped together by rods of iron or copper. The dam functioned for at least a thousand years, transforming the plain into a vast fertile garden of nearly a thousand hectares; it

South sluice of the Marib dam; from both north and south sluices water was directed through a complex network of channels to irrigate Marib farmland

The walls of the ancient Minaean city of Ythill, today's Baraqish

was said one could walk for four days continuously in the shade of the orange groves.

Perhaps the most mysterious of the four principal kingdoms was that of Ma'in. The Minaean civilisation was centred on the depression northwest of Marib known today as al-Jawf, its existence initially dependent on agriculture, its prosperity ultimately resulting from the caravan trade of which the Minaeans became the principal guardians. Their main centres were at Ma'in (ancient Qarnaw) and Baraqish (ancient Ythill). Towards the end of the fifth century BC, with the growing importance of the caravan trade, they fought their way to independence from Saba. The trade consisted mainly of aromatics – spices and cosmetics as well as incense – mainly from India; but the valuable frankincense and myrrh, increasingly in demand in Egypt as well as the Graeco-Roman world, was from southern Arabia

and the Horn of Africa. A Minaean colony was established far away in the north-west of Arabia to protect the route, and Minaean inscriptions elsewhere refer to trading contacts with Gaza, with Egypt, with Phoenicia.

Baraqish is the most accessible of the Minaean sites; others are in more disturbed tribal areas. The great walls of the city are visible from several kilometres away, rising out of a vast gravel plain. They average eight metres in height, including fifty-seven bastions, built of finely hewn masonry several stones of which are inscribed with the names of the kings who commissioned them.[23] The Italians have excavated the remains of a temple dedicated to the Minaean god Nakrah.[24] Much of the ancient site is covered by ruins of the medieval settlement when Baraqish was reoccupied by local tribes.

Qataban also managed to shake off Sabaean

hegemony around 400 BC, expanding its territory from its central focus at Timna' in Bayhan, south-east of Marib, as far as the Indian Ocean in the south. Timna', now known as Hajar Kuhlan and situated at the northern end of Wadi Bayhan, was the principal city. Excavation by an American team in 1950–51, revealed its walls, temples and residences – perhaps some of the sixty-five temples Pliny reported (not, however, from personal experience). Inscriptions on the walls include the laws of the city and other texts by the rulers, while an inscription on King Shahr Hillal's obelisk, which juts above the ground in the supposed market place, describes the commercial regulations. Qata-

ban's greatest prosperity seems to have been in the second or first centuries BC but fractious tribal relations have prevented more recent excavation.[25]

Linguistically as well as geographically Qataban was separated from the neighbouring kingdom of Hadhramawt by the great Wadi Mayfa'ah. Hadhramawt included the Wadi Hadhramawt and adjoining wadis, and also the coast at Qana protected by the towering black rock known as Husn al-Ghurab or Castle of the Crows. The kingdom was centred on Shabwah at the western end of Wadi Hadhramawt, less well watered than Saba or Qataban but benefiting from its proximity to ancient salt mines (spoiling their

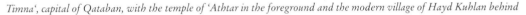

Timna', capital of Qataban, with the temple of 'Athtar in the foreground and the modern village of Hayd Kuhlan behind

drinking water, as Nigel Groom points out in his *Frankincense and Myrrh*).[26]

Hadhramawt's prosperity in the late first millennium BC was due to its ownership of frankincense growing areas to the east, mainly in what is now Dhofar in south-west Oman. Most of the incense was probably brought by sea from Dhofar to Qana and there transferred to camel-back for the journey to Shabwah. The trade was not all one way of course; amphorae from Gaza have been excavated at Qana, perhaps used for bringing the olive oil and wine for which Gaza was so famous.[27]

Shabwah (Pliny's Sabotha) is a bleak spot today, 'a distant place to which the sharp imagination of a tired man might adventure by the light of a dying fire in some bivouac of the night,' as the Master of Belhaven wrote in *Kingdom of Melchior*, 'a city forever beyond the hills.'[28] But it was well known to classical geographers – Strabo and Pliny as well as the anonymous author of the first century AD *Periplus of the Erythraean Sea*. The latter was a nautical man, from all the evidence, and the *Periplus* must have been an indispensable mariner's guide to the Red Sea and Indian Ocean. Inhabitants of the three villages on the Shabwah site have moved to a village nearby and their original houses, many of them re-using ancient stones, destroyed. But the little Burayki shrine (its white dome like a beacon to travellers arriving from the desert) has a large inscription embedded above its door, mentioning Yada'il Bayyin as king of Hadhramawt.

The site is now a tantalising field of stones, walls peeping out from beneath mounds of rubble. St John Philby, motoring there from Saudi Arabia in 1936, was much ruder than Belhaven, writing

Shabwah: aerial view of the main, north, gate and associated buildings, the largest thought to be the fortified palace of the Hadhrami kings, known as Shaqr

34

in his *Sheba's Daughters*, 'Of all Sheba's daughters the shabbiest, like a harlot in old age, poor and vicious and mean, the passing years have ravaged her youthful charm, the beauty of her prime has perished utterly, as if it had never been.'[29] He might think differently now: Shabwah's buildings, mainly dating between the first century BC and the fourth century AD, have been extensively excavated by French teams since the 1970s – temples, storerooms (or tombs?), residences and a large tower building, perhaps a palace that may be a prototype of the tower houses that are such a feature of Hadhramawt today. Shabwah is regaining some of its historical mystique.[30]

Each of these kingdoms, prospering on a foundation of superior agricultural technology, created a sophisticated religious and commercial culture to be seen in their sacred architecture and masterpieces of sculpture. At least sixty religious sites have been discovered so far in Yemen and some excavated. Worship was based on a male god who appears under various names – Ilmaqah in Saba, Wadd in Ma'in, Sin in Hadhramawt – often represented as a bull. The god's female partner was the sun goddess Shams (the meaning and the word preserved in modern Arabic); their son 'Athtar, god of irrigation and fertility, was the male form of the Babylonian goddess Ishtar, the Phoenician Astarte, the star Venus. Animal sacrifice prevailed, the blood caught in shallow stone offering tables often decorated with ibex or bulls' heads: to this day it is not uncommon to see a pair of horns attached to a house to ward off evil, or picked out in coloured stone on a façade. Incense was used in temple ceremonies and as offerings, judging by the number of incense burners found in excavations.

Temples were set within sanctified areas, usually

Sabaean alabaster head, the eyes outlined in obsidian. National Museum, San'a

outside towns, known variously as *hawtah, haram, mahram*, which often became the focus of pilgrimage, as at pre-Islamic Mecca and probably at Marib. At Shabwah a central avenue runs through the city to a monumental stone staircase leading to a four-column propylon and a huge pedestal, probably for a colossus in human form; behind is the city's main temple, dedicated to 'Athtar; the sixty temples mentioned by Pliny may in fact have been massive storerooms for gathering the incense for the annual caravan. Temples were built of finely dressed stone; one generally entered through a monumental propylon into an arcaded courtyard at the further end of which a flight of steps led through a pillared portico into an inner sanctuary roofed with stone. While most excavated structures at Marib date to the seventh century BC

Opposite: *Shabwah: Temple of 'Athtar beneath the city's southern wall*

37

or later, that of 'Arsh Bilqis ('throne of Bilqis' and traditionally thought to have been a palace) appears to have been built on earlier structures and pottery has been found on the site dating back to the end of the second millennium BC.[31] Brian Doe in *Monuments of Arabia* notes the influence of the classical Mediterranean world on South Arabian architecture, the 'translation of carpentry into stone' which so well describes the austere and unadorned architecture of these South Arabian structures, which are severely geometric and char-

acterised by monoliths whose only deference to decoration is shallow rectangular etching round the top of the stone.[32] The ground plan, based on the simple courtyard house, is not so different from that of the earliest mosques.

Other temples have been excavated at al-Sawda and Baraqish in al-Jawf, and at Huraydhah and Raybun in Hadhramawt. Fewer secular buildings have been found so far (apart from the probable tower palace at Shabwah, see pp. 34–5); sometimes, as at Old Marib, present-day occupation precludes excavation. Structures are often impossible to date accurately because the stones inscribed with the names of the original builders were sometimes misleadingly re-used in later structures.

Cult furniture found in association with the temples and in cemeteries include offering tables, pedestal altars, bronze bowls and inscribed dedicatory bronze tablets; these were attached to the walls of the courtyard or sometimes used for its paving. Thousands of votive heads have been unearthed, mostly of alabaster, their eyes inlaid with semi-precious cornelian and lapis; some are so finely carved as perhaps to have been portraits, and so might be signs of later contact with a wider world. There are also bronze statuettes; a particularly fine one in the National Museum of a smiling bearded young man (left), dressed in a lion skin, is dated by its 'boustrophedon' inscription (written as an ox ploughs – left to right, right to left) to the sixth century BC. And there are of course incense burners. By far the largest cache found so far was located in the great Awwam temple at Marib first excavated by the Americans in the 1950s.

Although the use of incense, particularly for embalming, is recorded in Egypt as early as the third millennium BC (and especially with the celebrated expedition despatched around 1500

Bronze statue of Ma'dikarib, c. 6th century BC, from the Awwam temple at Marib, now in the National Museum, San'a. He is bearded and wears a lion skin; a dagger is tucked into his belt on which are two inscriptions, one of which records his name, the other, in boustrophedon style, the dedication. Note the resemblance of the dagger tucked into his belt, to the daggers worn by Yemeni tribesmen today

THE ANCIENT KINGDOMS IN THE EAST

BC by Queen Hatshepsut to the much debated 'Land of Punt', most recently placed in Uganda),[33] early use in Mesopotamia and the Near East was probably mostly from local trees. The land route and the trade in sweeter and more efficacious resins developed on the back of the camel. The real craze for incense in the classical world seems to take off from around the fifth century BC; the upward movement of the smoke and the heady fragrance encouraged a sense of spirituality, and also disguised the foul smell of animals being roasted after the sacrifice and before the ritual feast, or even the stench of human cremation. 'Who is this that cometh out of the wilderness like pillars of smoke, perfumed with myrrh and frankincense, with all the powders of the merchants?' sang the author of the Song of Solomon. The two most valued commodities were frankincense (gum resin from the *Boswellia* species) and myrrh (gum from the *Commiphora myrrha* shrub); the latter is more common but was more prized in the ancient world than frankincense. Frankincense trees are now limited to Dhofar in Oman (and a few in Hadhramawt, Mahrah and Soqotra) but may earlier have been more widespread; Pliny maintained that it was grown in Qataban. There are however other aromatic gums grown in the Horn of Africa to this day and sold on the pavements of San'a – though none as heady as the frankincense of southern Yemen and Oman.

Much of our knowledge of the trade (and the traders) is derived from Greek and Roman accounts that have survived either in their entirety or as quotations in later works. The Greek geographer Strabo noted severely in the first century BC that it was necessary to treat accounts of southwest Arabia with indulgence, 'for not only is it furthest away from us but not many of our people have seen it' and much of what was reported was

The black volcanic outcrop of Husn al-Ghurab, with ruins of ancient Qana in front of the rock

from hearsay. Pliny the Elder, 'a man of insatiable curiosity and wide interests,' writing his *Natural History* in the first century AD, depended entirely on other authorities. It was he who maintained that only certain families of Hadhrami priests were allowed twice a year to milk the frankincense trees. 'Those persons are called sacred,' he wrote, 'and not allowed, while pruning the trees or gathering the harvest, to receive any pollution either by intercourse with women or contact with the dead.'[34]

Depending on the fortunes or otherwise of the Sayhadic kingdoms, the favoured route for the incense rade was by sea from Dhofar to the Hadhramawt port of Qana, extensively excavated by the Russians and more recently by the French:[35] it was here, on Husn al-Ghurab, a flat-topped black volcanic cone erupting from the beach, that in 1835 a British sailor, Lieutenant Wellsted, made the first discovery of a major

Inscriptions at Hasan-Ghorab in Arabia.

The first South Arabian inscriptions to be copied by a European, by Lt James Wellsted on Husn al-Ghurab (Wellsted, Travels II*)*

South Arabian inscription.[36] Qana was also used by Graeco-Roman fleets crossing the Indian Ocean from the second century AD. From Qana the caravans moved inland past the majestic city of Mayfa'ah, now known as Naqb al-Hajar, which protected the routes to the interior that led either to Timna' or to Shabwah. The heavy taxation exacted at the latter explains why Pliny assumed it had to be a city of at least sixty temples; in fact the rumoured temples now appear to have been vast store-rooms where the incense was accumulated during the year. From Shabwah the main

caravan set off once a year, thousands of camels together, along the desert fringe perhaps to Timna', Marib, Ythill/Baraqish and then continuing on northwards. By the first century BC the incense was taken on by the Nabataeans past Petra (more taxation), and eventually to Gaza, some 1,700 miles in all, taking perhaps 150 days.

Thanks to Arnaud, Halévy and Glaser and their collections of texts, the epigraphers, or better still palaeographers, were the first foreign scholars to grapple with South Arabian civilisation, whose complex legal and administrative systems they elucidated from thousands of mostly Sabaean texts. After a hundred years of work, the consensus is that the earliest inscriptions date from the mid-eighth century BC; but the fact that they are so finely written presupposes as yet unknown precursors. The languages are described as either Sayhadic or non-Sayhadic; the *musnad* script is usually written right to left but early ones are written 'boustrophedon'. Remnants of the languages may be preserved in the Mahrah region, in Dhofar in Oman and in Soqotra, known collectively as 'modern south Arabian'.[37]

The languages of South Arabia fall into two groups: one including those of the peoples of Hadhramawt, Qataban and Ma'in; the second and more widespread those of Saba, whose language was closer to northern Arabic. By far the largest number of Sayhadic inscriptions comes from the kingdom of Saba; there are fewer Minaean inscriptions although they are scattered widely – some have been found in Egypt, in Mada'in Salih in north-western Saudi Arabia, in Palestine and on the island of Delos. Hadhrami texts are rare and mostly confined to Wadi Hadhra-

Opposite: Mayfa'ah (today's Naqab al-Hajar), the main centre of ancient lower Hadhramawt, was also visited by Wellsted. According to an inscription, a city governor built the walls in the 3rd century BC but suggested the king of Hadhramawt should maintain them. Note the inscription on the left of the entrance to the city

mawt and Shabwah. Sadly there are few historical references among them, nor do they tell us much about the spice and incense trade. Although they are undated and undatable, they must be almost exclusively from the eighth century BC onwards. One inscription, however, (now in the National Museum in San'a) found at Sirwah, one of the two principal Sabaean cities, commemorates the construction of an enclosure or a palace by the Sabaean ruler, Karab'il Watar, a ruler mentioned in an Assyrian text of 685 BC.

The great problem for researchers is slotting the texts into some kind of chronology; the rise and fall in the fortunes of these tribal groupings does not help and the potential for disagreement is still enormous. Round about the beginning of the Christian era, with the rise of the Himyarite kingdom in the highlands north east of Aden, precise dating becomes more feasible. An approximate chronology has been devised, dating the Sayhadic kingdoms from around 700 to 110 BC, with two phases: the Sabaean domination between approximately 700 and 500 BC, followed by Minaean and Qatabanian autonomy between 500 and 110 BC, at which point Sabaean hegemony is once again asserted. Around the beginning of the Christian era the central highland tribe of Himyarites brings chaos to the region and introduces a period, to around 300 AD, of varying fortunes. By the first century AD Pliny is already describing the Himyarites as 'the most numerous tribe.' By threatening the rich agricultural base of the Sabaeans the Himyarites undermined the whole economic structure of Saba, which was also affected by the development of an alternative trade route through the highlands, guarded by such garrison towns as San'a and Sa'dah.

These changes had a limited impact on the caravan route; indeed Shabwah continued to flourish until its destruction, probably by the Himyarites, in the mid third century AD. An interesting aspect of Shabwah's culture is that both Hellenistic and Persian influences can be discerned on fragments of carved stone and on objects from this period. Greater contact with the outside world was partly due to the expansion of the sea route to and from India, with Aden as its chief entrepôt.

Arabia's contribution to the commodities of the aromatics trade was locally produced frankincense and myrrh. But there were many other aromatics that came from India and were as easily transported by sea. The Indian aromatics were carried on the winds of the south-west monsoon to Aden, known to the Greeks as 'Eudaemon Arabia'. Alexander is said to have contemplated several invasions of Arabia, including the southwest; he died before he could do anything about it but it was probably around this time that the Greeks became aware of the frankincense and myrrh which were to become such a feature of the Hellenistic world. Although the Greeks post-Alexander knew of the monsoon, it was the Romans who really exploited it to satisfy the growing appetite of Roman citizens for the spices and aromatics it supplied. The incense lands became known as Arabia Felix, by contrast with Arabia Deserta in the north, and an expedition (recorded by Strabo) was even launched by Augustus in 24 BC to conquer them.[38] The attempt was a disaster; the Romans under Aelius Gallus did manage to capture Baraqish mainly because the population rushed out of the city to fight them, leaving the Romans to slip in through the walls behind them (a funerary stele of a Roman soldier was found there, now in the National Museum in San'a). But the expedition foundered soon after, defeated by the desert. More and more of the aromatics trade was sent by sea, transshipped at Aden, offloaded

The new Marib dam, largely financed by Shaykh Zayid Al Nahyan, President of the UAE and descendant of tribes displaced by the collapse of the ancient dam in the 6th century AD

onto camels at Red Sea ports such as Berenice for the relatively short and well-watered desert crossing to the Nile, and then sent downriver to Alexandria and the markets of the Mediterranean.

While the loss of the caravan trade seriously undermined the prosperity of the desert kingdoms they were also affected by the internal wars resulting from the encroachment of the Himyarites on the territories of Saba, Qataban and Hadhramawt. The Sabaeans brought the Minaeans back under their control around the second century BC, but civil war had meanwhile split the state of Qataban with two provinces, Himyar and Radman, in the west and south breaking away in due course to form a new state, Himyar-Radman. The saga of tribal warfare repeats itself again and again in Yemeni history. Marib became a major religious centre again around 200 AD, as attested by numerous dedicatory texts and a revived coinage, but the political hub of the region was now in the highlands. Excavations have established that the temples of the area continued to be used up to the fourth century AD, only being abandoned with the advent of monotheism. The most crucial factor for the prosperity of these communities was the maintenance of costly irrigation works, in particular the vast Marib dam which is likely to have been breached on a number of occasions. It is said finally to have burst around the middle of the sixth century AD. Fields turned to dust and the local population scattered far and wide; some got as far as the south-east coast of Arabia, but all passionately preserved through genealogy their link with the south-west. Imagine the vision of Shaykh Zayid Al Nahyan, ruler of the shaykhdom of Abu Dhabi in the south-east (and President of the United Arab Emirates), fourteen centuries later, when he decided to spend some of his new oil wealth on rebuilding the dam and once more harnessing the mountain waters for Marib farmers. We may soon walk again for four days in the shade of the orange groves. And incense is still the characteristic aroma of every Arabian house.

III ANCIENT KINGDOMS IN THE CENTRAL HIGHLANDS

The village of Zafar lies south of the town of Yarim in the central highlands, on the edge of a shallow basin of well cultivated fields, watered by narrow canals that have channelled rainwater from the low surrounding hills. Here in the first century BC the rulers of the South Arabian kingdom of Himyar, first mentioned in inscriptions in 25 BC, developed their capital, the metropolis of a state whose territory was mainly in the central Yemeni highlands but which in its heyday extended further north, south, east and west. Zafar itself lies at an altitude of some 3,000 metres. It is a surprisingly peaceful scene today. Small stone houses cluster on the fringes of fields; women call to each other as they weed the crops of sorghum, barley and wheat; children hurry to and from the neighbourhood school, a contrast to the millennia of tribal disputes which have characterised much of the region's history.

Initially Himyarite autonomy depended on Sabaean weakness. Tribal upheavals on the eastern plain in the last two centuries BC facilitated the rise of the Himyarite kingdom in the highlands in the second century BC, a precarious rise however, always vulnerable to constantly changing tribal loyalties. Beautifully inscribed stelae record a succession of battles between Himyar and Saba, Himyar and Qataban, Saba and Hadhramawt, but at its peak in the third and fourth centuries AD the Himyarite kingdom extended not only northeast to the desert but also southwards to Tihamah, to Aden and the Bab al-Mandab, giving the Himyarites control of the narrow straits through which ships heading to and from India had to pass. A new approach to history begins here, for we now have a calendar, devised by the Himyarites around 115–110 BC.[39] By around 190 AD a Himyarite ruler is recorded as establishing himself as ruler in Marib. By the end of the third century AD they controlled the Marib heartland, they had humbled Shabwah, and had taken over the incense port of Qana; ultimately they extended their rule over Tihamah and parts of Hadhramawt. Thus the Himyarites established a kingdom whose extent was much the same as today's Republic of Yemen. In 270 AD the ruler Shammar Yuhar'ish styled himself impressively King of Saba, Dhu Raydan, Hadhramawt and Yamnat. (Raydan was the area immediately round Zafar.)

As was the case for the people of the caravan cities, the economic wellbeing and hence the political stability of the Himyarite state depended on the management of irrigation networks (only in the southern highlands is there enough rain to allow wholly rain-fed agriculture). Neolithic and Bronze Age communities in the highlands had already developed rudimentary irrigation systems – dams, canals, cisterns – and the Himyarites

Opposite: *The ancient Himyarite capital of Zafar in central Yemen*

Opposite: *Part of the 150-metre Himyarite tunnel, which once carried water to the city of Baynun from the other side of the mountain*
Above: *Ancient ruins and modern buildings of Baynun village*

greatly expanded them. One of the most outstanding examples of their technology is at Baynun, not far from Zafar as the crow flies. Baynun itself was once a Himyarite city, destroyed by the Ethiopians around 525 AD; extensive ruins curving round the upper part of the Numarah wadi give an idea of its importance. Just beyond the ruins a sunken shaft indicates the end of a tunnel that once brought water through the mountain to the city. On the next ridge to the east there is another tunnel, 150 metres long and still intact: one can actually walk through it. The achievement was impressive enough to attract the attention of the great tenth century Yemeni scholar al-Hasan al-Hamdani: 'one of the Himyarite kings bored

through [the mountain of Baynun] so that a water course from the land beyond could be directed to the land of Baynun.'[40] Huge plaster-lined cisterns, often excavated deep into the ground, are found all over the highlands; they are most easily spotted if one follows one of the many paths that twist between fields and over lava flows. One of the largest of these cisterns is under the third century AD temple at al-Huqqah, near San'a.

The most satisfactory way to appreciate the intricacies of Zafar's irrigation is to approach the modern village through the fields of cereals (separated by narrow channels running with water in the rainy season), and then clamber up the steep hillside, past store-rooms excavated out of the

47

Above: *Cistern in the mountain-top village of Shaharah, lined and waterproofed with* qudad, *a mixture of volcanic ash and slaked lime*

Right: *Massive basalt remains of Himyarite fortifications near Shibam-Kawkaban*

rock, to the remains of the castle at the top. Cisterns, also carved from the rock, are lined with a mixture of volcanic ash and slaked lime known as *qudad* to form a waterproof coating, a mixture still found all over Yemen wherever long-lasting water-proofing is needed. The hill is strewn with boulders, some dressed, others *au naturel*: a characteristic of Himyarite forts is the huge blocks, often of forbidding black basalt, from which they are built.

Himyarite inscription serving as a lintel to a house in Kawkaban, near San'a

Zafar itself is a small village whose occupants will willingly point out the inscribed stones that have been re-used in the walls of their houses. An elderly 'Himyarite' will finally appear to let one into the little museum, a microcosm of Himyarite culture. There are the usual inscribed texts, one of which describes the renovation in 447 AD of a palace on a nearby hill. More striking are fragments of limestone, perhaps from a palace or a fort, carved with vine scrolls and acanthus leaves, evidence of those wider Himyarite contacts with the Graeco-Roman world established by the trading links via the Red Sea in the early centuries AD.

Similar motifs are incorporated in an early mosque at Sarha near Yarim, not far from Zafar. There are also bronze, copper and ivory objects, perhaps of local manufacture. More evidence is in San'a's National Museum, which has some fine examples of Hellenistic-style bronze sculpture. The most outstanding, literally, are pieces of two huge male statues, reconstructed in the main hall; here you feel as if you have stepped into a totally different world. In their standardised Grecian pose they represent the ruler Dhamar'alay Yuhabirr and his son Tharan. They were found in 1931 at Nakhlat al-Hamra, a Himyarite palace site south of San'a on the road to Dhamar. According to an inscription on the left knee of the younger man they were made by one Phokas, most likely a Greek from the Mediterranean working for a South Arabian master, and were dated to between 270 and 310 AD A similar range of cultural influences has already been noted in carved stonework and bronze sculpture from Shabwah.

A result of these wider links was the spread of monotheism in southern Arabia. Paganism in the highlands had traditionally followed a pantheon similar to that on the plain; a small temple excavated in the 1930s at al-Huqqah, some 20 kilometres north of San'a, and dated to the third century AD, was probably dedicated to the same celestial pantheon as existed in Marib, Sirwah and Baraqish – moon, sun and the planet Venus. (After excavation the site was robbed for its stones but some of them may be seen in the walls of the nearby village.) The ground may have been made ready for monotheism by the adoption of dominant Arab deities, mentioned on various plaques and stelae, such as Rahmanan (as in the Arabic *rahman*, the 'merciful').

In 70 AD the Roman authorities destroyed the temple in Jerusalem, principal shrine of Judaism;

Relief carving of a pair of doves let into the wall of the Great Mosque in San'a, re-used from an earlier Christian building

this may account for the southward migration of Jews and the subsequent conversion to Judaism of Himyarite rulers. There is some debate as to which monotheistic faith came to Yemen first, Judaism or Christianity, or precisely when; clearly they were hard on each other's heels. Arab tradition puts the arrival of Judaism in the reign of Abikarib As'ad (*c.*430–450 AD) but conversion was well under way by the fourth century AD. Christianity was introduced to the Himyarites around the same time, possibly from Ethiopia, though the historical record mentions Bishop Theophilus Indus, summoned to the task from India by the Byzantine Emperor in around 342. Churches are known to have been built in Aden, in Zafar in 354, and in San'a where locals in the old city still point to a large round hole in the ground as the site of 'al-Qalis', built in the sixth century. Stones carved with certain Christian motifs are built into San'a's Great Mosque.[42] In 518 the last Himyarite king, Dhu Nawas, converted to Judaism and in 523, inspired by religious fervour or perhaps by

political design, massacred the Christian community of Najran in what is now south-west Saudi Arabia. Other Christians, notably the Byzantine Emperor Justinian, appealed to the Christian Ethiopians in the northern kingdom of Axum for help and an expedition was despatched under the general Abraha. Dhu Nawas was defeated and killed and Abraha established himself as governor in San'a, almost immediately declaring himself independent of Axum. Not for long, however: he got his come-uppance in 575 when he tried to capture Mecca and the Himyarites appealed to the Persians for help. One foreigner was replaced by another, a Persian governor ruling in San'a until central Yemen became part of the new Islamic empire in the mid-seventh century.

Judaism put down deeper roots than Christianity and Jewish communities were widespread in Yemen, despite periods of persecution, especially in the cities and southern towns. Some still survive in Yemen though with far smaller numbers since 1948–50 when the great majority of Jews migrated to Israel. There were said previously to have been some 50,000 Jews in Yemen as opposed to the two to three hundred who remain today. With their extensive network of international connections, especially in the Middle Ages, Jews played an important role in the economic life of medieval Yemen as well as later. But they were also intermittently persecuted, particularly in the seventeenth century when they were first expelled to the small Tihamah town of Mawza' and subsequently only allowed back to an area outside the city, Qa' al-Yahud, or Jews' Plain in San'a. Their freedom was circumscribed by regulations such as limitations to the height of their houses (which they circumvented by digging out deep basements, where they could brew alcohol). The German traveller Carsten Niebuhr noted some 2,000 Jews in San'a in 1763, celebrated for their craftsmanship in gold and silver and protected by the Imam in return for a small annual tribute.[46] In the nineteenth century it was his interest in the Yemeni Jews that brought Joseph Halévy to Yemen.

San'a has been the principal city of south-west Arabia for nearly two thousand years. Legend has it that it was founded by Shem or Sam son of Noah (the story of Shem is like a South Arabian Genesis, as Mackintosh-Smith puts it[43]), and its strategic position between Jabal Nuqum on the east and a higher range of hills on the west marked it out for settlement from the earliest times; one day archaeologists will be allowed to dig into the tell on which the castle stands. The name San'a itself may mean 'well fortified.' It is first mentioned in inscriptions of the first century AD, as a major garrison on the highland route between north and south, and by the third century it was a second capital to Zafar, a major market and commercial as well as military centre. By the fifth century at the latest San'a had probably replaced Zafar as the Himyarite capital. It was more central and guarded what was already a recognised trade and pilgrim route to Mecca, whose sacred stone attracted pilgrims long before it became the most sacred city in Islam.

The importance of San'a in the Arabian context was demonstrated by the palace, known as Ghumdan, built by its Himyarite rulers. Ghumdan, as Lewcock and Serjeant point out in their *San'a: an Arabian Islamic City*, was 'celebrated in Yemeni national ethos as an expression of the grandeur and both technical and aesthetic achievement of the ancient pre-Islamic civilisation.'[44] It was said to have been anything from ten to forty storeys high; its four sides were of different coloured stone, and there were copper or bronze lions at each corner which roared when the wind blew. The palace may have been demolished to make way for the Great Mosque in the seventh century. There are very few other signs of the pre-Islamic city to be seen in San'a today. It is virtually impossible to excavate in a living city, and all one can do is study the occasional inscription, some of them built into the walls of later buildings. Already in 1836 Lieutenant Cruttenden noticed an inscribed stone being used to cover a hole in the roof of a mosque.[45]

Today the local municipality, with some help from tourists and foreign aid workers on limited budgets, has begun to revitalise the old city of San'a and offset the drift of its inhabitants to the new suburbs. A UNESCO conservation programme has played an important part in preserving some of the public buildings but the continued well-being of the old city is inevitably precarious.[47]

Really to grasp the extent of the Himyarite achievement one has to roam slowly over the central highlands, dotted with fortresses whose foundations they laid, many of them guarding

Medieval fortified gateway to the town of 'Amran, with inscribed Himyarite stones embedded in the walls

so-called *hijrah* towns where fighting is forbidden and tribal disputes settled. At 'Amran north of San'a Himyarite stelae and inscriptions are built into the seventeenth century walls and entrance gate; along the escarpment beyond Kuhlan monumental masonry is impressive evidence that the Himyarites were there. They worked with the typical skill of the Yemeni mason whose handiwork has already been glimpsed at Baraqish and the Marib dam and at the many temples in the Jawf area; here in the highlands he is setting a high standard for future generations. But be warned: to many Yemenis 'Himyar' is an honorific used to describe anything of forgotten but ancient origin.

What we think of as Yemen today was still in the early Christian centuries – and would remain for several more – a collection of tribal states of constantly changing territories, each guarded by ferocious fortifications. It's not always easy to distinguish their ruins from natural fortifications of craggy rocks: looking out from the remains of the castle guarding Zafar itself, for instance, over the fields and nearby hills – which of the hilltops are man made? In many cases ancient structures have been re-used and rebuilt over the centuries, and cannot be visited because they have always been and still are military posts; the citadel at San'a for example, built on a tell that tantalisingly smothers evidence of the city's early history, is still a prison. Nevertheless history mingles easily with the modern world and the Himyarites are integral to the modern Yemeni's sense of identity and nationalism.

IV SAN'A AND THE COMING OF ISLAM

In the early seventh century AD Yemeni emissaries approached the Prophet Muhammad when he was in Madina to ask for instruction in the new form of monotheism which he claimed to have received from God via the angel Jibril (or Gabriel). The Prophet is said to have described Yemenis as 'the most amiable and gentle-hearted of men.' 'Faith is of Yemen,' he allegedly said, 'and wisdom is Yemeni.' Such an accolade was for a long time greatly to Yemen's credit; the modern state of Saudi Arabia recognized Yemen as the one country to have voluntarily converted to Islam and until the Gulf war of 1990–91, when Yemen was perceived as backing the wrong side, Yemenis were allowed to visit and live in Saudi Arabia and work there without visas or work permits. Yemeni tribes were conspicuous in the Islamic armies that in the seventh century swept across north Africa and into Spain where they settled in large numbers and where place names, tribal names and vocabulary have links with Yemen.

In 628, Year 6 of the Muslim *hijrah* calendar (a lunar calendar of which Year 1 is the year the Prophet fled from Mecca to Madina), the Persian governor in San'a, Badhan, was converted to Islam, allegedly by the prophet's cousin and son-in-law 'Ali ibn Abi Talib. Several of the Prophet's companions are said to have been sent to Yemen by Muhammad, and one of them may have built the mosque at al-Janad, a few kilometres north of Ta'izz, which often disputes with San'a the honour of being the oldest in Yemen. The whole of south-west Arabia was now nominally part of the new Islamic community, although, as we shall see, conversion was slow and needed reinforcement in the ninth century. Muhammad is known to have appointed a governor to rule in his name, who was responsible for the construction of the first Great Mosque in San'a and whose successors were appointed by the ruling dynasties in Damascus

Opposite: *The old city of San'a, according to legend founded by Noah's son Shem; much is of medieval origin*
Below: *Isma'ili women praying in the mosque of al-Janad*

The city walls of San'a, recently restored in the rammed earth, or zabur, *technique, are nearly three metres thick at the base*

and Baghdad. In the meantime Islam was probably followed mainly in the towns.

So what of this ancient city of San'a? Visitors, Arab and European, have always been impressed by its fortifications, architecture, and gardens, and by its populousness – around twelve thousand in the early seventeenth century, up to forty thousand in the mid nineteenth century and around one million today). 'Abounding in good things,' wrote the twelfth century Arab geographer al-Idrisi, 'and full of buildings … the oldest, the largest and most populous city of Yemen' – of Arabia, he could have added – 'an even atmosphere, a fertile soil, and the heat and the cold there are always temperate.'[48]

San'a is basically a medieval creation, and many of the houses pre-date the nineteenth century, especially in their lower storeys. The organisation of the city is typical of the region: massive perimeter walls (heavily and recently restored), a large and thriving market, a Great Mosque for the larger congregation on Fridays, and a ruler's palace, now

long gone but likely in the earlier period to have been near the Great Mosque. Such a palace typically included administrative offices, reception salons (usually with fountains playing in the summer), baths and well-watered gardens with more fountains.

The Great Mosque was said to have been built in the lifetime of the Prophet. Some sixty-five pre-Islamic columns were incorporated into the original fabric and it may have been built on a pre-Islamic site. In plan it follows the pattern of the simple courtyard house such as Muhammad's own house in Madina, which was the first mosque in Islam. Some of the present structure dates from the eleventh century when it was expanded and enriched by the Isma'ili Queen Sayyidah. The façade of the prayer hall and of the small domed building in the courtyard (which dates from the seventeenth century) are decorated with bands of black basalt. The minarets are early thirteenth century, the one on the south-west the typical combination of sections – square to cylindrical to hexagonal to small domed turret – that many other of the city's more elaborate minarets subsequently copied.

Alongside the Great Mosque is the principal market area, run strictly according to a series of regulations dating from the medieval period. Camel or donkey caravans would head for one of the many warehouses, or *samsarahs*, on the fringe of the market, that acted as a combined warehouse, hostelry and stable. One samsarah has recently been renovated and from its roof one can see how the whole city was organised: the market itself, with samsarahs round the edge, small watch-towers atop the selling areas to look out for thieves, and the residential quarters beyond, grouped round neighbourhood mosques. Near today's silver suq is Suq al-Mizan (with pre-Islamic masonry in its walls), so named for the scales – *mizan* – once used to weigh all goods prior to taxation; nowadays it is sacks of coffee beans and their husks that are weighed on gigantic scales. Suq al-Zabib is full of raisins, *zabib*; from time to time the grapes, grown widely in the area round San'a, have been used to make wine, despite repeated prohibitions by the Imams and religious teachers. One of the busiest parts is the textile suq; striped cloths from Tihamah, tie-dyed face masks (*maghmuq*) from San'a, futah skirt cloths from al-Shihr on the south coast hang alongside Gujerati silks and Chinese synthetics, testimony to Yemen's longstanding eastern trade links. The cloth merchants have often acted as money changers, their overseas dealings familiarising them with the world's currencies.

Samsarah (caravanserai) of Muhammad bin al-Hasan, founded c.1668-69; looted in 1948 it is badly in need of restoration but is a fine example of the decorative brickwork of the period

The market is still the economic and social heart of the old city, complete with craft, wholesale and retail businesses. There is nothing elegant about it, apart from the dilapidated samsarahs so badly in need of conservation. But the spirit that motivates it, the bustle, noise, crowds, the piles of enticing goods are endlessly fascinating.

The neighbourhood mosque would have been the principal building in its allotted quarter, with its all-important water for ablutions, for latrines and baths, and for the surrounding houses. Mosques are usually built of stone, their exteriors severe while interior decoration includes elaborate plaster work and sometimes painted designs. (It is not easy however for non-Muslims to enter any of the city's mosques.) Their minarets, mostly brick built, are conspicuous against the skyline, characteristic brick patterns highlighted with gypsum plaster. A few are older than the seventeenth century; some date from this century.[49]

Houses are typically tower houses, most of them five storeys high, some of them more. The lower third of each is stone, with burnt brick for the upper floors. Windows are glazed and topped by semi-circular *qamariyyah* ('moon-shaped' or 'moon-coloured' elements) filled with coloured glass; round ones are still sometimes filled with the translucent local alabaster. Externally, windows and decorative brickwork are highlighted with whitewash. Inside, five weary flights of steep stone steps (men must shout out to warn female inhabitants of their presence as they climb up) lead to the *mafraj* at the top, the grand viewing chamber, built to catch every whisper of summer breeze and of course the panorama (but not while chewing: qat does not agree with a breeze, say the experts).[50]

The pits from which the clay had been excavated for building bricks were then converted into vegetable gardens (called *miqshamah* from the

Above: *A moment of relaxation beneath a typical window of coloured glass set in a gypsum frame*
Opposite: *Shoe shop in Suq al-Milh in the old city, one of the main thoroughfares of the market*

white radish and horse radish *qushmi* popularly grown in them) belonging to the mosque, watered and fertilised by effluent from the mosque's ablution area or baths; they give a miraculous and unexpected sense of space to the old city. Vegetables and herbs are harvested daily, among them the popular basil, *rayhan*, which among its many properties keeps away the evil eye: men stick sprigs in their turbans; women use it to keep away flies;

bodies are covered with it before burial.

Water for the city was provided by an intricate network of canals, known as *ghayl*, that can still be followed from the surrounding hills (or could, until the recent surge of suburban construction in the 1990s following unification). Other water came from wells, their long inclined planes dug deep into the earth and buckets drawn up – several at a time – and tipped into channels. A main drainage channel through the middle of the old city, the Sayilah, was dug to draw off flash flood water (*sayl*) from the city, which it certainly does: a heavy storm in the rainy season can make it impassable for a few hours. Recently it was extensively lined and paved. West of the Sayilah the city developed round a series of palaces from the end of the twelfth century, in the area now known as Bustan al-Sultan, surrounded by gardens watered from the Sayilah. Subsequent palaces erected by Zaydi Mutawakkil Imams were rebuilt several times between the city and the well-watered 'garden district' known as Bir al-'Azab; one twentieth century palace now houses the National Museum. Bir al-'Azab, already a trendy suburb in the eighteenth century, was developed further in the nineteenth century, and adorned with magnificent villas by the Ottoman residents. Beyond that is the Jewish quarter, Qa' al-Yahud, vacated now by its Jewish inhabitants but characterised by narrow alleys of small houses noted in their heyday for their cleanliness. Deep basements were excavated to provide extra living space.

Europeans visiting San'a from the early seventeenth century onwards were generally impressed by its fortifications ('very curiouslie made,' said John Jourdain in 1609 of the city walls, 'for being

*A typical vegetable plot (*miqshamah*) in Harat al-Wadi in the middle of the old city of San'a*

Rain water in the Sayilah, main drainage channel of the old city, relished by these young local residents

earthe … 12 foote thicke and to outward showe is as fair as a stone wall'), architecture (fine buildings of lime and stone), gardens and palaces.[51] Cruttenden in 1836 was much impressed by the baths, still regularly indulged in, 'a favourite resort of the merchants who meet there to discuss the state of trade and the news of the day over their cup of keshr [*qishr* – infused husks of coffee beans] and their never-failing hukkah.'[52] Niebuhr, some seventy years earlier, was full of enthusiasm because he was given a proper bed to sleep in after a sad and wearisome journey: while critical of their general accommodation he wrote of one of the houses they visited that it 'was full of lovely rooms and was surrounded by a garden containing all sorts of fruit trees seemingly growing wild … a garden in the Arab style, with fountains and pools

and where one sought the shade rather than walked in the sun.'[53] He was also impressed by the splendour and warmth of his reception by the Imam. The prosperity of Sanʿa in 1763 was evident in the markets overflowing with fresh fruit and vegetables, textiles from all over the Indian Ocean (accounting for the well-dressed inhabitants), streets for every conceivable trade and craft.

To walk in the old city is an intense pleasure at any hour of the day. Early in the morning, at the dawn call to prayer, to hear it chanted by a cacophony of rival voices from the minarets whose decorators were also surely trying to outdo each other in the immaculate interlacing patterns on their shafts; later, to see the market come to life, cramped stall holders unfolding themselves, Toyota trucks offloading mounds of alfalfa near the now

Men buying qat for the afternoon's chew; the women are draped in sitarahs *and tie-dyed face masks or* maghmuqs

vanished Bab al-Sabah, tomatoes, monstrous watermelons and of course bundles of qat, the vendors pausing for a breakfast bowl of beans from steaming cauldrons in pavement eating houses. At midday in the narrow streets of residential areas, to smell fresh bread, cooking meat, while women wrapped in vivid tablecloths known as *sitarahs* hurry home with bundles of fresh vegetables and men brush past with their qat wrapped in pink plastic. After lunch, while the men relax in the mafraj to chew the qat and mull over politics, business and family affairs, to watch their children playing tiddlywinks in the street, flicking fruit stones into the indentations of manhole covers. After the afternoon prayer, the market is at its busiest, stallholders with cheeks bulging with golf balls of qat hawk spices from India and Africa, tinned goods from all over, piles of raisins from the nearby countryside; *janbiyyah* daggers previously (but no longer) with prized rhino horn handles, superb silver jewellery, lumps of coral and lapis and cornelian from foreign parts, the crowds jostling and bargaining as they always have done. Then with the call to the evening prayer, shutters come down, wooden doors are barred and the suq slowly goes to sleep while its inmates head for the mosque. The residential areas are awake late these days; electricity, television and the sleep-depriving effects of qat keep the lights on behind the multi-coloured windows and to walk then in the old city is like walking through a kaleidoscope, muffled voices adding to the mystery, and only dogs to keep one company in the alleyways. For this is their hour, the hour of the scavenger, and of the old neighbourhood watchman doing his rounds through the night.

San'a has experienced all the ups and downs of fortune that characterise the history of this corner of Arabia. That most notable foreign scholar of Yemen, Professor Serjeant, wrote in *San'a* of the recording of Yemeni history as an insufferably tedious and meaningless to and fro of battles and campaigns, with a broad pattern emerging of foreigners securing the lowlands and then invading the highlands, where the pattern was of organized rule round the family of the Imam alternating with tribal anarchy. Because of its position, control of San'a has always been essential to control of the highlands north, east and west, and has passed through the hands of a succession of ruling dynasties – the Yu'firids from the Shibam-Kawkaban area (847–998); Isma'ili Sulayhids with strong affiliations with the Fatimid dynasty in Egypt (in San'a 1047–1087); Hamdanids (1099–1173); Ayyubids, invading from Egypt (1123-1228). The Ayyubids and their successors the Rasulids finally melded Yemen into a single unit. Intermittently, from the tenth century until the Ottoman invasion in 1538, San'a was in the hands of the Zaydi Imams from the north. Under the Ottomans San'a once again became the seat of a foreign governor, the newcomers leaving their mark on the city with the Ottoman-style Bakiriyyah mosque in the east near the castle. Although the Ottomans were forced by the Zaydi al-Qasimi Imams to retreat from Yemen in the mid-seventeenth century, they still regarded it as part of the Ottoman Empire and re-occupied it again in the nineteenth century to ward off possible European incursion.

Traditionally the Imams built their private palaces outside the city, for security. The finest examples are just to the north of San'a – the great rock palace, Bayt al-Hajar (about a hundred years old), in Wadi Dahr, recently renovated as a government guest palace, and in the 'garden city' of al-Rawdah. A popular view of the Wadi Dahr palace is from the escarpment overlooking it; male guests of wedding parties cavort there on Thursday afternoons (weddings usually take place on Thursdays), performing the *bara'* dance if they

Bayt al-Hajar palace in Wadi Dahr near San'a built by Imam Yahya in the 20th century

Kawkaban: old houses and almond trees overlooking rain-fed cisterns

have had enough qat. Al-Rawdah was described in the seventeenth century as well supplied with splendid pleasure houses, fountains, delicate fruit trees and fish ponds. That German critic Niebuhr compared it with Damascus.[54] Much of its graciousness has disappeared today, wth only half-abandoned palaces as reminders of earlier pleasure grounds. But in spring it is enveloped in apricot and almond blossom, emulating the garden of Paradise in which every righteous Muslim ruler would wish to be seen.

The richness of the northern plain, as well as its strategic position, account for the continuity of San'a's history. The fertile volcanic loam, carefully terraced with low dykes, planted with cereals, vines and qat, is watered from wells and cisterns and guarded by diminutive watch towers. Environment, tribal tradition, religion – each plays its part in moulding the history of Yemen. Various sites in the central highlands illustrate the mixture. The partnership of Shibam-Kawkaban for instance, north-west of San'a, separated by a thousand-foot escarpment but connected by a finely constructed path: Kawkaban above on its clifftop ramparts complete with Himyarite inscriptions, as well as nineteenth century Ottoman fortifications and an access road built in the 1960s by Egyptian forces during the civil war that established the republic;[55] while Shibam below is the local commercial and religious centre, home base of the

Doorway of the 9th-century Great Mosque in Shibam, northern Yemen

Opposite: *Looking down on Shibam from the walls of Kawkaban on top of the escarpment;*
Thula lies at the foot of the hills on the other side of the plain
Above: *A mason at work repairing the elaborate brickwork of a house in Thula*

Yu'firid tribal dynasty that rose against the governors of San'a in the ninth century. It was they who shortly afterwards built Shibam's handsome mosque, famous for its painted ceiling, a decorative feature of several early Yemeni mosques. It may have been built on the site of an earlier temple; certainly there are Himyarite pillars are incorporated in market shops.

Another example of the historical and environmental mix is the fortified market town of Thula, a pre-Islamic and medieval settlement, headquarters of an unsuccessful revolt in 1590 against the first Ottoman occupation, whose leader, Imam Qasim al-Mansur, was commemo-

rated in the early twentieth century with a hecatomb commissioned by Imam Yahya, leader of a successful revolt against the second Ottoman occupation. Elsewhere the fortress of Dhu Marmar has frowned over the Marib road north-east of San'a since pre-Islamic times; in caves below a curious cache of fourth century mummies was found in1983; the medieval fortress, built on Himyarite foundations but now much ruined, must have played an important role in the fortunes of the Bani Hushaysh people, whose fertile fields and vines extend below. Or – one last example – the remote hilltop settlement of Zafar Dhibin, its fine sixteenth century mosque, commissioned by

67

Above: *Minaret of the 16th-century hilltop mosque of Zafar Dhibin, its fine brickwork reminiscent of medieval Iranian work*

Right: *The small cubic mosque of Masjid al-'Abbas, at Asnaf in the Khawlan, is richly decorated with carved, painted and gilded patterns, here on the wooden coffered ceiling*

Imam Qasim al-Mansur, whose actual tomb lies within, indicative of an importance one would never guess nowadays. It is difficult to know where to stop in a landscape everywhere so visibly marked by millenia of history.

V ZAYDI IMAMATES IN THE NORTH

Opposition to the foreign domination that features from time to time in Yemeni history has often been based in the northern highlands, an ill-defined region beyond the strongly fortified market town of 'Amran, extending from the hills above the escarpment in the west to the great wadis of al-Jawf in the east. The region is often known as *bilad al-qaba'il*, land of the tribes; tribal loyalties are strong in this area though not always dependable beyond the confines of one's own tribe, as the last Imam of Yemen, Imam Badr, found to his cost in the civil war of the 1960s. Strangers from outside the tribe are regarded with suspicion, sometimes hostility, the wariness reinforced by a fundamental conservatism combined with a fervent Islam.

Rainfall in this area is lower than further south. Heading north from San'a, as the landscape changes from moody volcanic hills to dry, wide pastoral valleys, it is easy to understand how architecture in Yemen harmonises so fundamentally with the landscape. Stone houses yield to mud towers, the mud applied not as bricks but as distinctive layers, known as *zabur*, which are upturned at the corners, giving a house a faintly oriental look. Doors and windows are framed with bands of paint coloured red, white or yellow from local minerals.[56] Houses are still huddled together, partly to leave as much space as possible for the cereals, legumes and vines of the local economy, partly for security. Tribal rivalry is intense and even fields are guarded by watch towers, especially when planted with precious qat. Small boys herd sheep and goats with slings.

Palaeolithic and Neolithic sites have been discovered in the region around the main city of Sa'dah, but exploration is not easy. Sa'dah is an ancient settlement, ideally placed for the assembly of caravans, including the annual caravan of pilgrims heading to Mecca. There are iron mines and gold workings nearby.[57] The settlement itself was celebrated as a tanning centre and also for the finest wine, for its horses, good seed fruits, grapes and livestock. The hills around Sa'dah are crowned by forts, one of which, al-'Anba, was used in the civil war of the 1960s; it is reached by an ancient track with South Arabian inscriptions etched in the rock face beside the path. The route northwards to the Hijaz was guarded by another great castle some sixty kilometres north of Sa'dah, Umm Layla, a group of mountain-top defences dating from the early centuries AD and used right through to the 1960s, when it was another major royalist stronghold. Again there are South Arabian inscriptions on huge blocks of masonry, and a network of medieval and later fortifications – storehouses, mosque, citadel as well as the all-important cisterns

Opposite: The 17th-century bridge, built across a sheer and deep gorge at Shaharah, a Zaydi stronghold in northern Yemen

Umm Laylah in northern Yemen, a longstanding fortress guarding the caravan route

still well water-proofed with qudad.

Sa'dah came into its own in the 890s when two attempts were made to bring Yemen back into the Islamic fold from which it had seriously lapsed. Endless tribal disputes led to an invitation to a certain Yahya ibn Husayn ibn Qasim al-Rassi living in Madina to come to settle the squabbles. His first effort failed but he returned in 897 and set up an Islamic base in Sa'dah, declaring himself Imam by right of descent from the Prophet through Zayd ibn 'Ali, great grandson of 'Ali, husband of the Prophet's daughter Fatimah (genealogy is a much used historical tool in Arabia). Zayd's branch of Islam had been established around 740 in Iraq. Thus was founded the Yemeni Imamate, subsequent members of which were descendants of the sons of 'Ali (al-Hasan and al-Husayn) and the rightful rulers of the country until their removal in the 1960s.

Al-Hadi Yahya was a man of legendary physical strength; it was said that he once grabbed a galloping camel by the tail, the hump and the rear remaining in his hand while the head and front legs raced over the horizon. He was also a man of great learning, the author of forty-nine books, some of them still used by Zaydi theologians, and a distinguished poet, a skill greatly appreciated in the Arab world. The form of Islam he brought to Yemen is known as Zaydi Shi'ism. Apart from the Zaydi devotion to 'Ali and its insistence on the institution of the Imam, there is little to distinguish it from orthodox Sunni Islam. There is however a geographical distinction, with Zaydi Islam prevailing in the northern area – at least as far south as Dhamar south of San'a – and reinforced by the innate conservatism of the tribes who adhere to it; this accounts to some extent for the greater wariness towards non-Muslims who are rarely allowed

The minaret and two of the many domes of the 9th–14th century Great Mosque of Sa'dah, which houses the tomb of Imam al-Hadi Yahya, surrounded by those of his descendants

inside a Zaydi mosque. Sunni Islam, known in Yemen as Shafi'i for its adherence to the school of Imam Shafi', prevails in the south and in Tihamah.[58]

Al-Hadi Yahya is buried in the Great Mosque of Sa'dah, surrounded by eleven of his descendants.

Their domed tombs, remodelled in the later medieval period, are reminiscent of the carved domes of the Mamluk rulers of Egypt, in the cemeteries of Cairo, an alien touch compared with the great tower houses nearby. The Great Mosque is a courtyard mosque like that of San'a

Tower house in Suq al-Inan in northern Yemen, built in the zabur (rammed mud) technique, windows highlighted with paint from local minerals

and most Yemeni mosques, and the present buildings date from the twelfth century, although they were extensively altered and enlarged in the seventeenth century. Most unusually, its minaret is in the middle of the courtyard. It is still the centre of Zaydi teaching.

The old city of Sa'dah is a supreme example of mud architecture, almost all of it, including its walls, built in the rammed earth or zabur technique. Walking round the walls or through its cavernous streets overshadowed by tall zabur houses one has the sense of trespassing in a forgotten world. The walls of the houses rake slightly inwards and windows are picked out in elaborate

lime plaster decoration, as are the roofs, which rise in horns at the corners as if in deference, even in this heartland of conservative Islam, to that ancient symbol of power, the bull. A toy Ottoman citadel inside the main gate, Bab al-Yemen, sits on as tantalising a mound as the citadel in San'a; it is easy to imagine the unhappiness of its nineteenth century Turkish garrison, surrounded by hostile and treacherous tribesmen. Alongside is a baker of the army bread, a small round loaf known as *kidam* made of flour and ground lentils introduced by the Ottomans. It lasts at least a week — small consolation for a beleaguered garrison who must have longed for access to a freshly baked loaf.

The Imam was elected from among the descendants of the Prophet, qualified also by learning, piety, generosity, military prowess and administrative skill. Often the succession was disputed – there were after all vast numbers who could claim descent from the Prophet – but sometimes a son was chosen. Sometimes there was no candidate at all, and government was left in the hands of tribal shaykhs. The Imam's power base was always the north of the country but in later centuries it was recognised that control of San'a was essential if his rule was to be extended southwards.

To reinforce his legitimacy the Imam depended on the *sayyids*, members of a religious aristocracy scattered throughout the countryside, also claiming descent from the Prophet. They too could qualify to be elected Imam, and their support was therefore not always reliable. In 1948, a group calling itself the Free Yemenis, or *Ahrar*, and mainly composed of members of the sayyid class, was responsible for the assassination of Imam Yahya.[59] In general, however, they provided the intellectual élite and much of the pre-unification bureaucracy in the north. Other respected members of society are the *qadhis*, judges, upholders of Islamic law. Both sayyids and qadhis are often recognisable by their silver and gold caps (*imamah*) and immaculate dress. They also wear particular types of dagger (*thumma*), worn to the right rather than in front.

Until recently society in the north had changed little since pre-Islamic times, and it was a valuable field for anthropologists. Even today society remains organised along tribal lines, with the tribesman, *qabili*, wearing his *janbiyyah* dagger jauntily over his navel as he strides over northern town and countryside, regarding himself as bound by a concept of honour that includes the right to bear arms; outside the city he is likely also to have a gun over his shoulder. The heads of tribes, the shaykhs, are elected from families in whom the office is hereditary. Tribal dress is distinctive: a short gathered skirt rather like a Scottish kilt, traditionally a black and white goathair waistcoat over a shirt, today a shabby version of a western jacket, handwoven shawl tossed over shoulder or wound round capped head. It is worn with a panache that suits the stride of someone who is used to walking from place to place, even if he is also the owner of a Toyota pickup.

All southern Arabian tribes are said to be descended from Noah's son Shem through Qahtan

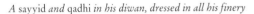

A sayyid and qadhi *in his diwan, dressed in all his finery*

Evening view of the mountain-top village and white-washed mosque of Shaharah

(Joktan in the Old Testament) but such common ancestry has never made for harmony except in the face of foreign invasion. In the region north of San'a are congeries of fractious tribes that generally belong to one of two great tribal federations – Hashid and Bakil – but their territories are interwoven and give rise to endless land disputes. These are often settled by shaykhs sitting in so-called *hijrah* towns, neutral territory with a long pre-Islamic history. The shaykhs often employ tribal custom or *'urf*, rather than Islamic law, in settlements. Tribesmen in theory give undivided loyalty to the tribe which gives its protection in return.[60]

The Imam had forever to be on his guard against tribal lawlessness, his authority seldom extending beyond the main towns. The endemic disputes from time to time descended into anarchy, until a strong enough Imam was found

76

to pull the tribes together again, often by managing to appeal to a sense of higher national unity. This was the case for instance in 1598 when Qasim ibn Muhammad, a descendant of al-Hadi Yahya, claimed the Imamate with the title *al-Mansur Billah*, victorious by the grace of God. A sort of Robin Hood, he had a series of miracles to his name in battles against the Ottomans, sallying out from mountain bases at Shaharah and Dawran (south of San'a): a remarkable woman poet, Fatimah bint Muhammad Ahmad wrote of the impregnable fortress of Shaharah in 1702 as 'home of all grace! Shaharah is the head and none can approach its loftiness …higher than the slender neck and fairest brow.'[61]   Dawran was sadly the epicentre of the 1982 earthquake which added to the ruination of what must have been a splendid palace; bits of its decorative plasterwork are strewn about its devastated salons. Qasim ibn Muhammad was also responsible for the mosque of Zafar Dhibin, on a hilltop north of San'a, where he and his son are buried (see p. 68).

For over a century the Qasimi family produced some remarkable Imams to govern Yemen, but always against a background of tribal challenge. One of the better known, thanks to the pen of Carsten Niebuhr to whom he gave so warm a welcome, was al-Mahdi 'Abbas, son of an African slave mother, according to Niebuhr, who wrote that he was 'gorgeous and disorderly but of impressive grace and generosity;'[62]   he was described by a contemporary Yemeni scholar, al-Shawkani, as perspicacious, intelligent, a strong manager, high-minded – what more could one want?[63]   Niebuhr considered San'a a paradise, with courteous and hospitable inhabitants, well-stocked suq and magnificent buildings, one of them the tomb the Imam built for himself, the handsome Qubbat al-Mahdi. His successors were less notable, however,

being unable in the early nineteenth century to defend Tihamah against incursions by the fiercely puritanical Wahhabi warriors from central Arabia. Wahhabi disruptions in the Hijaz, around Mecca and Madina and further south into Yemen, led eventually to an Egyptian expedition, at the Ottomans' request, since both the Hijaz and Yemen then were still regarded as part of the Ottoman Empire. 'Turco-Egyptians', as Professor Serjeant aptly called them, remained in control of Tihamah until the 1830s.

The resulting chaos in the highlands, with a series of Imams unable to shift the intruders, led ultimately to the second Ottoman occupation. In 1849 the Turco-Egyptians captured Hodeida on the coast but were unable to assert control over the highlands until the 1870s. San'a was repeatedly

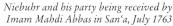

Niebuhr and his party being received by Imam Mahdi Abbas in San'a, July 1763

devastated by tribal attacks; Joseph Halévy, in between collecting ancient inscriptions, reported that half the buildings were in ruins and in 1905, when Imam Yahya besieged the city, the inhabitants were reduced to eating cats and dogs.[64] Even Tihamah was under constant threat from the tribesmen of the Zaraniq tribe, notorious over the centuries for their refusal to accept outside authority, as well as for their piracy along Yemen's coast. In the late nineteenth century another remarkable Imam came to the rescue, Muhammad ibn Yahya Hamid al-Din. Echoing his ancestor by reviving the title *al-Mansur Billah,* he became the focus of a nationalist revolt against the second Ottoman occupation, this time from a base in Sa'dah, thus effectively uniting the principles of Zaydi doctrine with Yemeni nationalism.[65] It was his son, Imam Yahya, who ruled an independent northern Yemen after World War I until his assassination in 1948.

The Zaydi city of Sa'dah has none of the bustle of San'a or Ta'izz; instead the alien visitor feels shunned, watched by invisible eyes. Even the suq, with piles of grapes and pomegranates in season, raisins at other times, is subdued by comparison with San'a; there is a sense that the locals despise commerce.

A few Jewish craftsmen squat on the ground, the remnants of their beautiful silverware spread in front; they mostly live in a couple of villages not far from Sa'dah, members of a once thriving community. Jewish Yemenis or Yemeni Jews? The controversy arose when Israel persuaded some 50,000 of them to migrate in 1948–50, in an operation known as Magic Carpet. The truth lies somewhere between: some are descendants of the original diaspora (Yemeni Jews), but the majority are likely to be descended from indigenous converts. Some 20,000 Jewish silversmiths migrated to Israel; sadly there are today as few practising their craft in Israel as there are left in Yemen and examples of the exquisite lace-like necklaces for which the crafts-

Well-armed local tribesmen at the Saturday market of Suq al-Talh

*A boy reclines with his Kalashnikov
in the back of a pick-up at the
Suq al-Talh market*

men were so famous are difficult to find.[66]

The busiest market in the area, typical of the weekly markets which take place all over Yemen, is on Saturdays at Suq al-Talh, some thirty kilometres to the north, notorious for its gun trading. Some of the bargaining was carried on until recently in Maria Theresa thalers, the handsome heavy coins prized for their reliable silver content. Tribesmen armed with the Kalashnikovs essential to the tribesman's *amour propre* wander among stalls selling the brilliantly coloured women's dresses and nylon brassières. But fruit and vegetables are also for sale, piled up in huge rubber tyres while foreigners buy the multi-coloured traditional straw baskets in which the fruit used to be sold.

These weekly markets are organised on a tribal basis. The market area is declared *haram* – sacred – where fighting is forbidden. Some markets are held in local towns, others in specially designated spots such at Suq al-Talh, others named after the day on which they are held – Suq al-Khamis, for instance, on the fifth day, i.e. Thursday, at the northern end of Tihamah. They are still held all over the country, social and economic focuses for every community.[67]

Moving westward towards the escarpment one comes to appreciate the skill with which the Yemeni farmer uses to the utmost the terrain and the limited rainfall, easing the latter through his fields when it comes, letting it rest for a while in one shallow terrace before releasing it to the next. To a Muslim water is a sign of divine concern; he gains credit, for instance, if he provides a public supply for passers-by to use and it's not unusual in the Yemeni countryside to find a roadside tank, today perhaps a jerry can, with mug, with which to help oneself to the precious contents. In Hadhramawt the water supply may be housed beneath a little whitewashed dome known as a *siqayah*; in cities like San'a the public drinking fountain, or *sabil*, is everywhere.

Machinery is ill-suited to the terrain; the farmer ploughs by hand and donkey, occasionally humped ox or a camel. Cairns mark boundaries and are sometimes dressed with a frill of fabric – a scarecrow? or perhaps propitiating some ancient god? Fields are planted with red and white sorghum, maize, wheat, barley, legumes such as lentils or fenugreek, the latter for the healthy green slime, *hilbah*, that tops the lunch dish of saltah. The sorghum is harvested in stages: first the leaves are stripped for fodder, then the heads to be dried and ground for flour, finally the stalks, piled up in the branches of trees for later use as animal feed; pieces are sometimes wrapped in green alfalfa as a kind of lollipop for old women to feed to the family cow. Women work alongside men, singing as they cut with miniature scythes.

The plain is hemmed in on the west by mountains where a string of fortresses guards against the foreign invasions that feature so regularly in Yemeni history. The most dramatic of these is Shaharah,

A woman carries water from one of Shaharah's many cisterns

its famous bridge swung by some miracle over a profound gorge in the seventeenth century, allegedly by one Salih al-Yaman. Shaharah was a refuge and military base for Imam Qasim Muhammad. The steep masonry causeway up the mountain was defended at intervals but today only one small fort remains. There are cisterns fed by channels collecting rainwater from the hills. After a breathless climb one reaches the bridge itself, glimpsed first round a corner, then climbed down to and crossed via gates either end. The village was much ruined by Egyptian bombs during the 1960s civil war when it was again a royalist stronghold; a crumbling palace and small mosque are all that remain of its older heritage.

Heading west from the town of ʿAmran, heavily fortified by Imam Qasim in the seventeenth century and scene of a major battle in the secessionist revolt of 1994, the road passes several villages guarded by large round towers, acting as refuges in time of war. Other fortifications on the edge of the escarpment guarded routes between coast and plateau. Kuhlan on the way to Hajjah has already been noted for its outlying Himyarite forts; its own thirteenth century castle was a useful post overlooking a vital communication between ʿAmran and the northern Tihamah. Further on the same road is Hajjah, a provincial capital whose medieval castle is still a prison where even recently chains were rattled when visitors rang the bell. Again an Imamate stronghold in the struggles against the Ottomans, a much nastier prison deep underground housed a group of *Ahrar*, Free Yemeni conspirators accused of assassinating Imam Yahya in 1948; they became celebrated for their literary output during their incarceration.[68] Below the citadel is another fine, more comfortable castle.

The terrain and the climate change sharply between Kuhlan and Hajjah, their craggy heights

A young woman carrying a sack of coffee; drawn by Georg Wilhelm Bauernfeind, one of Carsten Niebuhr's companions on the Danish expedition of 1763

often enveloped in cloud that has swept up from the coast. The Chinese-built road, a remarkable piece of engineering in which several Chinese lost their lives (they are commemorated by an exotic oriental cenotaph by the roadside), hugs precipitous cliffs, overhanging the lush vegetation of wadi bottoms where banana and papaya flourish, butterflies and irridescent sunbirds dive in and out of hibiscus and hornbills honk in the dense foliage. There are even baboons, cousins of the Abyssinian species, flopping clumsily down the cliffs. The Ethiopian connection is also flashily maintained by the blue and russet plumage of the Abyssinian rollers. They are our introduction to the novel world of Tihamah whose torpid heat rises to greet us as we descend the escarpment.[69]

VI COASTAL TIHAMAH

The descent at any point down the escarpment to the Tihamah plain is precipitous and even the three or four roads that have been built are littered with the carcasses of unfortunate vehicles that failed to take the bends quite slowly enough. But from north to south the escarpment is densely populated, every crag topped by a village, every slope embroidered with terraces. On foot it is covered with paths and staircases connecting terraces with villages, villages with springs of clean water. In summer monsoon rains pour down the cliffs from cloud-covered peaks; standing at the top you look down on a sea of cloud as if from an aircraft. The rain is carefully channelled through terraces of coffee (at 1,000–2,000 metres) and qat, cascading into steep-sided wadis and eventually down to the farms on the plain. In the rainy season there are pools and waterfalls for children to play in but most water is laboriously harnessed for precious crops.

Jabal Raymah is a typical area of the escarpment, its small stone villages huddled on outcrops to leave as much space as possible for terraces. People bawl their news from rooftop to rooftop, from village to village. Life here is hardest on the women, some spending hours each day fetching clean water, others clambering up and down between terraces, planting, hoeing, weeding, harvesting. The men descend to the weekly market on the plain,

often the only place to buy essentials, and return laden up the precipitous paths at the end of the day.

The plain, some 450 kilometres north to south and some 30–45 kilometres wide, immediately calls to mind those ancient African links discussed in Chapter II. The Red Sea may be slowly but relentlessly widening but communication across it has been continuous and is particularly evident in Tihamah. Most important is the rain, blown across from the Ethiopian highlands, a mere 50 millimetres a year at the coast but as much as 500 millimetres on the escarpment. Human exchanges between Ethiopia and Yemen have occurred throughout the centuries; recent excavations at Sabr near Aden (not strictly Tihamah) have renewed speculation that given time archaeologists may find more evidence of links across the water; shell middens along the coast may lead to the discovery of other early settlements.[70]

Much of Tihamah was in Ethiopian hands from the third century AD, and it was the springboard for their invasion of the highlands in 525 AD, when the Ethiopians came to the rescue of local Christians after the massacre at Najran in 523. From at least the ninth century, under the Ziya-did founders of Zabid, the African link was sustained by trade, the principal commodity being slaves for the Imam, for tribal shaykhs, for agriculture, for the army. All over the Middle East

Opposite: *Fishermen mending nets at Yemen's main port of Hodeida*

*Thatched 'ushshah, a traditional Tihamah
house, in a family compound
at Mahal al-Ha'arib*

armies consisted mainly of slaves, or mamluks (*mamluk* = being owned, enslaved), in Yemen's case particularly from Sudan. In the eleventh century the Najahid dynasty was founded by an Ethiopian slave, Najah, and the Najahid ruler Jayyash is said by one authority to have established the town of Hays, now noted for its pottery. And in the eighteenth century the amir of al-Luhayyah, as Carsten Niebuhr noted, was entirely black, brought to Arabia and sold to a local notable: 'we found him to possess the dignified politeness of a nobleman, the strictest integrity and the candid benevolence of a true friend.'[71] The most profitable import from Ethiopia has of course been the coffee plant

but another delicious import is the Yemeni sourdough pancake, *lahuh*, a version of the Ethiopian *injera*, served either with ghee and honey or with a sauce of yoghurt and chopped herbs.

One British historian – Professor Rex Smith – has written of Tihamah as a region 'of truly incredible discomfort seemingly for all but the local inhabitants.'[72] I disagree but recall camping beneath a heavy canopy of stars, sweating in the Tihamah night (even in January), bitten by a thousand tiny black flies and aroused in the middle of the night by a terrifying encirclement of local hounds howling in unison from surrounding dunes. In the morning there is no such thing as refreshing sunrise; the sun rises hot and high, awakening bees in stacks of hives. The Tihamah plain is hot and humid all year round.

Tihamah has two roles. One is trade, at different periods through one or other of its three ports: Hodeida, Yemen's main port although Aden, Yemen's second city, is now rivalling it; al-Luhayyah, north of Hodeida, now only a small fishing village; and Mokha of coffee fame but now dilapidated and largely deserted. Internal trade is carried on through the ancient city of Zabid and such market centres as Bayt al-Faqih and Bajil at the foot of the mountains.

Tihamah's other role is agricultural. It has always prospered from its produce but especially during the Rasulid period, the thirteenth to fifteenth centuries, when elaborate star almanacs were drafted to regulate the farmer's year.[73] The seven major wadis flowing out of the escarpment bring both surface water and aquifer replenishment to the richest agricultural region in Yemen, stretching some 25–30 kilometres from the escarpment. Shallow terraces formed by at least two thousand years of silt deposit are separated by metre-high dykes, rebuilt every year and making a mosaic-like pattern across the plain, interspersed with lines of date palms and papaya. As the countryside grows flatter, the lush vegetation of the lower escarpment yields to fields of cotton, sorghum, sesame, maize and the sweetest melons. Tihamah is a palette of sharp flavours and strong colours, as in the brilliant striped cloths woven in Bayt al-Fakih or the chillies in the saucer at mealtimes.

Many of the inhabitants of the plain live in villages of immaculate reed dwellings known as 'ushshah, close cousins of the African hut, made of mud, mixed with chopped straw, and palm fronds, some round and conical, some rectangular with elaborate roof ridges. Sorghum stalks and mud

daub form the windowless walls, held together by ropes. Some of the finest are on the banks of the two northern wadis, Wadi Mawr and Wadi Surdud, where the houses are grouped into compounds. An extended family will occupy a brushwood walled compound containing several straw huts, carefully allotted to different family members and uses: reception, cooking or storage for instance. Wooden frame string beds – *angarib*,

A family inside the 'ushshah, whose walls are decorated with colourful paintings and enamel plates from China

similar to the Indian charpoy – are for sleeping as well as sitting; floors are of spotless mud plaster, reworked every week. Such architecture, based on available materials, is found either side of the Red Sea. House interiors are often decorated with intricately painted designs – flowers, calligraphy, topical objects such as cars, aeroplanes, guns – and objects from all over the world, most strikingly perhaps gaudily painted enamel plates from China. Women in these villages or in the fields are unveiled, revealing faces that are clearly a mixture of African and Arab.[74]

Crowning a few of the villages are magnificent brick fortresses belonging to shaykhly families (Tihamah is as tribal as the highlands). One of the grandest is al-Rafi'i in Wadi Mawr, dominating the surrounding village, richly decorated around the upper storey; another is at al-Dhahi, built in 1934.

By far the most distinguished town in Tihamah is Zabid, on the western edge of the agricultural belt, serving historically as Tihamah's agricultural centre and as trade centre. Tihamah history is marked by uprisings of local tribes against rule from the highlands; Zabid was founded in one such uprising about 820, by the Ziyadids, a dynasty whose founder was despatched by the 'Abbasid Caliph in Iraq to quell unrest in Yemen. The Ziyadids ruled Tihamah, often through Ethiopian deputies, for most of the ninth and tenth centuries. Zabid's heyday came some time later, however, with the Ayyubids and their successors the Rasulids from the end of the twelfth until the middle of the fifteenth centuries. The Rasulids were intent on maximising their taxation revenue, establishing a strong centralised administration for its collection, and collating agricultural almanacs to increase farming revenue from the Tihamah and the uplands. Their exactions were so ruthless that it was said no man who owned a date palm could

afford to find a wife.[75]

In those days Zabid was also an important centre for indigo dyeing, the indigo grown extensively in Tihamah, cooked in huge clay vats and beaten into cotton cloth with wooden mallets to produce the irridescence that made the cloth so highly prized. Niebuhr in the eighteenth century found huge vats of it fermenting outside the town but nowadays a chemical equivalent is imported for the colour so favoured for turbans and dresses in the highlands. The dyeing process is elaborate and painstaking, the dyers stained blue by their efforts. But they are surely worthwhile: how about a tribesman in an indigo-dyed turban with a brilliant green splash of basil tucked into its folds for a stylish demonstration of Yemeni panache?

Medieval Zabid served not only as the Rasulid winter capital (summers were spent in cooler Ta'izz) but also, thanks to their patronage, as a centre of religious and scientific learning. Libraries and schools were founded to teach students from within Yemen as well as overseas. Eighty or more mosques and *madrasahs* are said to survive out of the 230 mentioned during the Rasulid period, even if the academic reputation has dwindled.

The great Moroccan traveller, Ibn Battuta, was captivated by Zabid, noting its luxuriant gardens 'with many streams and fruits.' 'The pleasantest and most beautiful town in Yemen,' he wrote. 'Its inhabitants are charming in their manners, upright and handsome, and the women especially are exceedingly beautiful.' The women made a great impression: describing festivities attending the date harvest, when everyone, including women in litters on camels, left the town, Ibn Battuta added, 'For all we have said of their exceeding beauty they are virtuous and possessed of excellent qualities.' They were even prepared to marry foreigners – he must have been tempted.[76]

A woman from northern Tihamah whose face reveals a clear blend of African and Arab

A massive Ottoman gateway leads through old walls into the town's main square. On one side of the square against the outer wall is the Ottoman fort (built as usual on earlier foundations) while a substantial mansion houses the local governor. A huge fig tree in the centre shades the local café patronised by local literati sitting or lying on angaribs. Down narrow alleys high whitewashed walls and devious entrances hide from the stranger the elaborately decorated mansions within. Houses face on to cloistered courtyards, a flight of steps leading to the main entrance set in a façade decorated with ornamental brickwork and stucco. Inside an extraordinary wealth of decoration and ornaments provides a kind of resumé of trade and travel links, for Zabid is no backwater. Such domestic architecture is typical of that found all along the Red Sea as well as in Ethiopia, where in

The 15th-century Great Mosque in Zabid, built over 12th-century foundations

the upland city of Harar, for instance, there are intricately carved stucco designs on every available space.

The suq winds through the centre of town. Industries associated with the suq include the production of sesame oil, still prepared in side alleys where blindfold camels turn the great sesame presses to extract the precious oil. The Great Mosque, north-west of the suq, is a typically Arabian building, unpretentious, simple and above all peaceful. Like Zabid itself it was founded in the ninth century by the Ziyadids, the present modest

buildings dating mainly from the fifteenth century. The climate demands plenty of shade and the mosque's small courtyard is surrounded by deep arcades, one of them stacked with string biers for transporting the dead from home to mosque to cemetery. The mosque and the adjoining madrasah are still the focus of the town's academic life, its spiritual and intellectual centre.

Zabid's suq is a model of tranquillity compared with that of market day in Bayt al-Faqih to the north. Every Friday this is the centre of Tihamah's commercial and social life, drawing mountain together with plain. *Faqih* in Arabic means learned, devout and the town derives its name, House of the Learned One, from the tomb of Ahmad ibn Musa ibn 'Ujayl, famous for his wisdom and sanctity in the thirteenth century. People settled round the tomb, hoping thereby to gain blessings and in due course this population attracted traders. The tomb is still visited on market days and the saint's day; such ritual visits, known as *ziyarah*, are a regular feature of life in Tihamah and in the Hujariyyah south of Ta'izz.[77] In the seventeenth and eighteenth centuries Bayt al-Faqih was frequented

Decorated plasterwork surrounds a Zabid doorway

89

by growers and buyers of coffee, a convenient half-way house between the terraces where it was grown and Mokha whence it was despatched around the world.

Bayt al-Faqih used to be famous for its cotton fabrics woven on handlooms around the town. Most of the textiles on display in the suq are actually woven now in San'a but still generally dyed in Tihamah. It is also an ideal place to study the range of womens' costumes, especially the tight-fitting, embroidered dresses; it is a treat to see the women so proudly displaying them, instead of covering their glitter with black *abayas* as in the highlands. A Tihamah woman often wears a headscarf under a small domed hat exquisitely

A woman selling henna in the suq of Bayt al-Faqih

crafted from tender doum palm fronds. But her face will be uncovered.

The pottery centre of Hays is south of Zabid and has been active for at least four hundred years. The pottery, mostly bowls, little coffee cups, water containers, is generally glazed green, yellowish or brown. The town was founded in the tenth century by the Ethiopian Najahid ruler Jayyash who, according to the fourteenth century traveller and commentator Ibn al-Mujawir, sent for his family and relations to come and settle in Hays. There was said to be not a single house of Arabs there, all of them being offspring of blacks.[78]

The fortunes of the ports along the coast have varied, thanks mainly to silting-up. Zabid for instance, some fifteen kilometres from the coast, seems to have had several ports of which the one most mentioned, Ghulayfiqah, is around thirty kilometres north of the nearest point on the coast to Zabid – not very satisfactory. This is not an easy coast. 'Navigation is dangerous along the whole coast of Arabia,' wrote the first-century AD author of the navigator's guide, the *Periplus*, 'with bad anchorages, foul, inaccessible because of breakers and rocks.'[79] Two ancient ports are mentioned in the *Periplus*, both at the southern end of Tihamah: Musa or Mawza', which has yet to be satisfactorily identified, and Ocelis, which is identified with Khawr Ghurayrah opposite the island of Perim. Later Arab navigators preferred the African coast where the reefs are less treacherous. Pirates were also a constant hazard, often members of the fierce Zaraniq tribe based in the Bayt al-Faqih region.

Al-Luhayyah, port of northern Tihamah, is said to have been founded in 1402, its harbour indifferent even when Niebuhr landed in 1763, with boats anchoring way off the beach. Nowadays it is in a state of terminal decline: a little boat

*Bayt al-Fakih is famous for its weavers, here
shown weaving typical striped cotton fabric*

building, a little fish drying, a few salt pans to the
south but overall an air of irreversible dilapidation,
accentuated by the half-collapsed buildings,
innards exposed to the elements, revealing
remnants of hidden glories. The principal building material is coral stone, a good building
material, used up and down both sides of the Red
Sea, but needing constant attention which al-
Luhayyah can no longer provide. The Ottomans

built a small fort on the edge of town, its aloof-
ness accentuating the loneliness of such outposts
of occupation, their homesick garrisons ground
down by boredom.

The track south passes al-Salif, with a flourishing
salt industry and now ferrying the occasional
tourist to the nearby Kamaran Islands a few kilometres offshore. These were occupied briefly in the
sixteenth century, first by the Mamluks from

The 15th-century mosque and tomb of Shaykh 'Ali ibn 'Umar al-Shadhili in Mokha

Egypt, later by the Portuguese who were attempting, unsuccessfully, to control the Red Sea, and then in the nineteenth century by the British who first – in their bossy but efficient way – established a quarantine station for Muslim pilgrims, and later an air base; the islands' original viability depended on the pearling industry, now to a small extent replaced by foreigners diving to admire the coral.[80] Further south, Hodeida came into its own in the nineteenth century, especially during the second Ottoman occupation when it was the main link between the rest of the Ottoman Empire and San'a tucked away in the highlands. The French were commissioned to improve the link with a railway, intended to cut the journey time to San'a from six camel days to one by train,

but politics and the escarpment blocked it.[81] Remains of some handsome stone houses, with rich plaster decoration and elaborately carved doors and windows, can still be found, not quite as collapsed as at al-Luhayyah but unloved and only precariously protected. The port was modernised by the Russians in the 1960s but today Hodeida is fighting off attempts by Aden to pre-empt its rôle as Yemen's chief port.[82]

Between Hodeida and Mokha a sea of sand separates irrigated agriculture from the Red Sea. A few small fishing settlements border the beach spreading out their catch to dry; several tantalising shell middens indicate the possibility of early Neolithic settlements, probably seasonal. Some boat building and a few palm groves can be seen, but there is little else until one arrives at Mokha, perhaps the saddest place in Tihamah. The town came to fame in the fourteenth century when a mystic, Shaykh 'Ali ibn 'Umar al-Shadhili, follower of the Shadhili *sufi* brotherhood, returned to Tihamah from Ethiopia allegedly bringing with him a coffee plant because, so he sensibly reasoned, he needed the coffee to keep him awake during his meditations. Shaykh 'Ali is as revered for his mysticism as for his coffee plant, hence the finely decorated minaret attached to the mosque built over his tomb in the fifteenth century. Sufism is deeply embedded in Islam, emerging in Iraq and Iran in the early centuries and in Yemen particularly in Tihamah with its connections via pilgrim traffic to a wide variety of Islamic practices. It has produced holy men of great stature as well as devotional poetry and music, absorbing traditions from Africa as well as from the east. Sufism also often provides a link with folk religion and superstition, hence the disapproval of the strictly orthodox, including the Zaydi hierarchy.

Mokha is miserable now, despite efforts to revive its port with concrete quays and cranes. It is hard to reconcile the few remaining nineteenth century buildings, the crumbling walls finely decorated in the Red Sea stucco tradition, with the descriptions of medieval and European merchants, the latter setting up there in the seventeenth and eighteenth centuries for the export of coffee. The coffee plant, known as *bunn*, flourishes best at a height between 800 and 2,500 metres, its bright red berries harvested in March–April and November–December. It is dried and the husk separated from the bean; the husk itself is infused with sugar and spices to provide qishr, commonly preferred by Yemenis, for the beans are expensive. Coffee itself, or *qahwah*, is imbibed in small delicate quantities, every sip carefully savoured. Exports

from Mokha may have begun in the fifteenth century, but it was the Ottomans who spread the good news further afield. By 1580 a Venetian visiting Egypt noted a hot black drink favoured by the Turks after meals, to be consumed with friends, rather as qat is today. However, at one time in Constantinople coffee was regarded with great suspicion, its sellers threatened with being sewn into sacks and thrown into the Bosphorus.

By 1600 Mokha was prospering on the proceeds and began attracting the attention of British East India Company merchants. Various British expeditions tried trading with Yemen via Mokha in the early seventeenth century, mainly to correct an imbalance in their trade with India; John Jourdain in 1609 found 'very faire buildings … and very populous as well of Arabs as strangers, merchants', among them a large community of Indians. There were 'about 35 saile of ships, great and small' from all over the Indian Ocean bringing all sorts of commodities, Mokha acting as the entrepôt which Aden had been and one day would be again.[83] In 1610 the English merchant Sir Henry Middleton had a much worse time, jailed by the local governor, despatched to San'a, returned to Mokha, where he was back in jail and escaped only by a miracle.[84]

The East India Company was unperturbed and established a factory there in 1618. By the 1660s coffee houses were sprouting in London and Paris; 'it so incloseth the orifice of the stomach,' ran a London advertisment, 'and fortifies the heart within, that it is very good to help digestion … it much quickens the spirits and makes the heart lightsome …' and more besides: irresistible.[85]

Competition for the bean was fierce. British merchants were helped by the colony of Hindu merchants known as Banyans. The Dutch established themselves in 1708, the French in 1706, the

Americans in 1803. The coffee was brought down from the terraces to the market at Bayt al-Faqih (Beetlefuck to disgruntled foreign merchants) and transported thence by its purchasers to Mokha – four camel days away. Central control of Tihamah was shaky at the best of times and foreigners in Mokha were at the mercy of local suspicion of non-Muslims, easily triggered if the governor was so inclined. Carsten Niebuhr and his companions came in 1763, several suffering from malaria, and were most unsatisfactorily treated. The British bombarded Mokha in 1820 after some particularly treacherous treatment of their merchants, compensating the town later with the establishment of a hospital.[86]

Sadly for Yemen, in 1711 the French had already bought some coffee bushes which they transplanted in Réunion, the Dutch also taking some

Basket-sellers in the market of Bayt al-Faqih, Tihama

Ruined minaret and warehouses in Mokha,
reminders of the coffee port's heyday

to Java. The coffee drinking world was thus no longer dependent on Yemen for its supplies. But already by the end of the eighteenth century and even more after Napoleon's attempt to gain control of the Red Sea through his unsuccessful invasion of Egypt in 1798, Europeans were showing a different sort of interest in the Red Sea. Surely it offered a swifter route to India than that via the Cape of Good Hope? In 1839 Britain acquired Aden; its far superior harbour and the development

of steam transport needing coal stored in Aden spelled disaster for Mokha. Nowadays, on a hot but windswept day, only a winter traveller, a lonely Caspian tern wandering on the grubby beach, and the name of Mokha/Mocca/Mokka on packets of coffee in the dusty corner store remind the passer-by of the travels and travails of Mokha's coffee merchants, the minaret over the Sufi master's tomb recalling the debt owed to this original transplanter of the precious bean.

VII THE SOUTHERN HIGHLANDS

A constant factor in Yemen's history is the Red Sea. In the Islamic period this water-filled section of the Rift Valley came to be regarded with special sanctity because it led to the holy places of Mecca and Madina. But it was also a major medieval trade route, coming into its own with the shift of power in the tenth century from the Baghdad of the 'Abbasids to the Cairo of the Fatimids, and later the Ayyubids and Mamluks. Each of them aimed to control the populous corner of Arabia that guarded the entrance and exit to the vast commercial world of the Indian Ocean at one end, Egypt and the Mediterranean at the other. Some of these foreign claimants to the control of Yemen ventured from the coast to northern areas via the southern highlands, often brought to a halt by the Zaydis just north of the great 2,800-metre Sumarah Pass.

The southern highlands are the greenest area of Yemen; at almost any time of year the terraces are covered with cereals, qat, fruit trees, watered by an average rainfall of around 800 millimetres a year. Towns such as al-'Udayn, Ibb, Jiblah, above all Ta'izz have prospered as market centres for agricultural produce, including the best coffee and, it is said, the best qat.

A steep ascent to the highlands, and one which highlights the shifting environment from coast to different altitudes of the escarpment, to the miraculous greenery of the southern highlands, is from the pottery centre of Hays. The track rises up past the wadis feeding into the great Wadi Zabid on the plain to al-'Udayn, famous for coffee grown on the terraces either side of the road. This is a lively town on the upper levels of the escarpment; it lies in a basin surrounded by terraced hillsides planted with coffee, qat and fruit trees. Niebuhr commented on the 'exquisitely agreeable perfume' of the coffee bushes in flower, planted on terraces like an amphitheatre. From al-'Udayn a narrow

Opposite: Rich, well-populated farmland in Wadi Bana, between Yarim and Damt; several crops per year can be grown on the ancient terraces
Below: Coffee bush in the southern highlands; when ripe the beans turn bright red

Jiblah market

road climbs another 800 metres to the top of the escarpment. Travellers pause at the top for the view, right across to the Red Sea on a clear day; so popular is the viewpoint that gipsy dancers provide indifferent entertainment to passers-by. From there it is only a short distance to Jiblah which with its sister town of Ibb dominates a wide basin green with cereals, so well-watered that farmers can reap several harvests a year. John Jourdain was much impressed in 1609: 'in this place they doe sowe their corne all times of the yeare, and doth yeild fruite every three months … for I have seene some corne sowinge, some reapinge, some ripe and some greene all at one time.'[87]

The first time the southern highlands significantly enter the medieval history of Yemen is with the remarkable Sayyidah bint Ahmad (sometimes known as Queen Arwa), daughter-in-law of the founder of the Sulayhid dynasty, with strong ties with the Fatimids in Egypt. The latter belong to the branch of Shi'a Islam that recognises as Caliph descendants of Muhammad's daughter Fatimah

(hence Fatimids). Missionaries began spreading the heterodox doctrine in Yemen from the tenth century; some of their tombs, deep in the Haraz mountains west of San'a, at such places at al-Hutayb, are still places of pilgrimage for Isma'ilis (the current term for most Fatimids) and Bohras (also of Fatimid derivation) from western India, the heady aroma of Indian incense revealing the pilgrims' origin.[88]

By the eleventh century the Sulayhid dynasty, established by 'Ali bin Muhammad al-Sulayhi and ruling from San'a, had won uneasy control over much of the north. The dynasty was constantly involved in tribal war. Sayyidah bint Ahmad became the Sulayhid leader after her husband, Muhammad ibn 'Ali, abdicated, allegedly because of ill health, in 1086. According to the contemporary historian 'Umarah al-Hakami, this remarkable woman 'was of fair complexion tinged with red, tall, well proportioned but inclined to stoutness, perfect in beauty, of a clear-sounding voice', and so on; her famed benevolence included restoring and expanding the Great Mosque in San'a. However, given the endemic tribal unrest, it was not surprising that, when pressed by the Zaydis, the queen decided to move her capital. At this point she asked her husband to assemble the people of San'a. 'Look at them!' she exclaimed (according to 'Umarah). 'What do you see?' Wherever he looked he saw only the flash of swords, the glint of naked blades. Then she took him to Jiblah and they summoned the people there. On all sides his glance met only men leading sheep or carrying vessels full of oil or honey. That was the place for her, she decided.[89]

Though supposedly founded by the Sulayhids, Jiblah has Himyaritic remains on the mountain behind the town, Jabal Ta'kar, where the queen's treasure is said to be buried. No one knows if this is really so because a military post keeps investigators at bay. Interestingly these remote garrisons with not a great deal to do have accumulated a remarkable collection of pre-Islamic objects occasionally on display in the Army Museum in San'a.

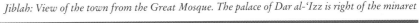

Jiblah: View of the town from the Great Mosque. The palace of Dar al-'Izz is right of the minaret

Jiblah is a town of great charm, built as usual up a hillside to leave space for fields. The huge dilapidated Dar al-'Izz is on the right as one enters, and is supposed to be the queen's royal palace; the present wobbling structure is certainly much later, but there may be Sulayhid foundations. The narrow street of the permanent suq leads to the congregational mosque founded in 1087. Of the original building probably only the southern minaret remains. The queen's modest tomb is in the prayer hall.

On the eastern side of the main road from San'a to Ta'izz is the larger town of Ibb, the old walled town now nearly submerged within sprawling bustling suburbs. 'This cittie standeth very pleasant and in a firtill soile,' wrote Jourdain as he passed through on his way to San'a, 'and very populous, and the land round aboute very well manured.'[90] Ibb has never been a capital (unlike Jiblah), and its prominence is due to agricultural wealth and its position on the trade and pilgrimage route between Aden and San'a and on

The 11th-century Great Mosque of Jiblah, containing Queen Sayyidah's tomb

Engraving after a sketch by Niebuhr of Ta'izz, showing the road to San'a on the left and that to Mokha on the right

northwards. Only the walls remain of its medieval fortifications; the citadel that housed the Ottoman garrison in the nineteenth century is outside the walls. Inside the gates – locked every night until the 1950s – its tall dark-stoned houses frown over alleyways, the large number of underground cisterns an indication of the town's ability to withstand siege. This it successfully did in 1904 when Imam Yahya tried to wrest it from the Ottomans.

One of Ibb's oldest mosques is the thirteenth century 'Asadiyyah, on the edge of the suq, restored on several occasions by the Rasulids. Inside are vestiges of the vivid painted decoration which once covered the whole interior. Once, when I was sitting outside Ibb's main mosque, the muezzin's loud falsetto rang out to declare the moment we had been waiting for – the end of Ramadhan (the Muslim month of fasting) – and suddenly windows and doors were flung open (like an Advent calendar was the un-Islamic thought), and from all directions people crowded round the eating houses and tea shops; qishr was already brewing, plastic bags of lemonade were being filled, samosas were flying to salivating mouths. Old Ibb came alive. But most activity today has shifted to the new town lower down the hill.

A much easier route from coast to southern upland than that via al-'Udayn leads from Mokha to Ta'izz. This may well have been the route taken by the Ayyubid invaders in 1173, led by the brother of Salah al-Din al-Ayyub (Saladin), Turan-shah. In despatching his brother to Yemen, Salah al-Din, based in Cairo, was asserting orthodox Sunni guardianship of Mecca and Madina, but also and more importantly control of valuable Red Sea trade. This was also the route taken by most European visitors from the sixteenth century onwards. The Ayyubids' emphasis on Sunni orthodoxy also included trying unsuccessfully to stamp out any vestiges of Fatimid doctrines in Yemen.

What is described as a vast army enabled Turan-shah to conquer Ta'izz, Aden and Jiblah, and ultimately to control the whole southern area as far north as Dhamar, establishing an administration that effectively swept aside local tribal dynasties. It is only with this Ayyubid conquest that one can begin to think of Yemen as a political entity. Fifty years later, in 1223, the then Ayyubid ruler of Yemen departed for Mecca, appointing one Nur al-Din 'Umar al-Rasul as his deputy. Five years after that Nur al-Din became the independent ruler of southern Yemen and Tihamah, founding his own Rasulid dynasty. The Rasulids were more readily acceptable to many Yemenis because of their alleged descent from

The late 13th-century Muzaffariyyah mosque in Ta'izz; its notable mihrab is just right of the modern minaret

Qahtan, father of all southern Arabs; the Ayyubids, to their detriment, could only claim descent from Adnan, father of northern Arabs.

The two centuries of the Rasulid period are generally recognised as the most brilliant in Yemen's history as well as the most prosperous (the country was probably richer than it is today), thanks to agricultural revenue from Tihamah as well as to profits from east-west trade passing via Aden.[91] The Rasulids were scholars, architects, poets and encouraged others of that ilk. We have already met them in their winter capital, Zabid; now it is time to meet them in their cooler summer capital of Ta'izz, still the most dynamic city in Yemen and virtually founded by the Rasulids. It climbs up the steep qat-covered slopes of 3,000-metre Jabal Sabir, and is described in the fourteenth century by Ibn Battuta as 'one of the finest and largest towns' in Yemen. However 'its people are overbearing, insolent and rude, as is generally the case in towns where kings reside.'[92] Through Rasulid control of Aden, trade flourished with both east and west, customs dues financing their beautification of Ta'izz with palaces, mosques, madrasahs and convents for sufi brotherhoods.

Most Rasulid buildings have disappeared; those that remain include the principal and exquisite Muzaffariyyah mosque (second half of the thirteenth century), its impressive façade and tower-like *mihrab* facing on to the modern town. It was built by a notable Rasulid ruler, Sultan al-Muzaffar. Two madrasahs are the 'Ashrafiyyah (1398–1400) and the Mu'tabiyyah (1392). Built on the lower slopes of Jabal Sabir, their minarets still stand out against the modern city; their domes are colourfully painted on the inside, an architectural feature introduced by the Ayyubids. To the Ayyubids both domes and madrasahs were demonstrations of orthodox, Sunni Islam.

General view of Ta'izz showing theRasulid walls and fortifications climbing up Jabal Sabir. The 14th-century 'Ashrafiyyah madrasah can be seen bottom left

Though no palaces are left, the medieval historian al-Khazraji has left a description of a splendid complex built in 1308–09 at Tha'bat in the Ta'izz hills.[93] This included a vast throne room with painted ceiling, surrounded by elaborate gardens aimed at imitating on earth the Paradise to which all good Muslims aspired and within which Muslim rulers liked to be seen. If Ta'izz were not growing at such a rate, archaeological investigation would probably reveal much more of its medieval heritage. For almost nothing remains of old Ta'izz

apart from fragments of fortification clambering across the slopes of Jabal Sabir and two gates, Bab Shaykh Musa and Bab al-Kabir, the latter leading into the suq. Ta'izz market is unique for the number of raucous women vendors, some selling qat which they have brought down from mountain terraces, others hawking balls of camel and goat cheese, a Ta'izz speciality. In the merchant-traveller Ludovico de Varthema's day, the early sixteenth century, Ta'izz was famous for its rose-water as well as 'all kinds of elegancies.'[94] There

Tomb of 'Abd al-Rahman ibn 'Awf, a Companion of the Prophet, in the Hujariyyah

is also a vast range of foreign goods, a demonstration of the city's connections with the outside world. These were effectively banned under Imams Yahya and Ahmad but burgeoned after the establishment of the republic.

With the demise of the Rasulids Ta'izz's importance somewhat waned. But in 1948, after the assassination of his father Imam Yahya, Imam Ahmad decided to make it his capital, in preference to rebellious San'a. He lived there until his death in 1962, in an undistinguished and uncomfortable palace that is now a museum of mid-century trivia ('gaudy gewgaws'), some superbly embroidered costumes and gruesome photographs of how Ahmad dealt with his father's assassins, now the heroes of the republic.[95]

Holy men (known as *walis*) are much revered in the countryside south of Ta'izz. One of the most famous shrines, on the slopes of Jabal Habashi, is that of Shaykh Ahmad ibn 'Alwan, who died in 1267 and is buried in the mosque of Yafrus. The present buildings, with madrasah attached, were commissioned by the Tahirids in the fifteenth century. It has become a sort of Yemeni

Lourdes, attracting the sick and especially the lunatic, rattling chains at the occasional tourist.[96]

Beyond Yafrus rises the volcanic massif of Hujariyyah (pronounced Hugariyyah), the well-populated heartland of Shafi'i Yemen, with its main towns of al-Turbah and Hayfan. The hills are dotted with the whitewashed domes of revered tombs, the reverence much frowned upon by Zaydis but sign of a lively popular faith in the south. You see it on saints' days – *ziyarahs* – throughout the year. Leading families of the Hujariyyah, their members often also commemorated in little white tombs, are regarded with an almost feudal respect, understandably so, since they are among the country's most prominent merchants and industrialists with a good deal of patronage at their disposal. Such families used to send their sons to be educated in Aden or even in India; others took themselves to work in Aden port, and it is remarkable today how many government ministers and bureaucrats, leading businessmen and merchants, come from that small area. Much of the industry that fringes Ta'izz was founded by that Hujariyyah elite.

Rasulid greed contributed to the dynasty's downfall in the mid-fifteenth century. A series of mediocre rulers besieged by squabbling family members allowed the Rasulids' fragile control of the north to weaken and by 1454 effective power had shifted to the Banu Tahir, whom the Rasulids had unwisely appointed as governors of Aden. The home base of this tribe lay in the south-east of the country, in an area which until unification straddled the border between the two Yemens. It is bisected by the Wadi Bana, a deep gorge with perpetually flowing water that debouches in the south into the great Abyan plain, a region wary of outsiders, bordered by Rada' in the north, al-Bayda

Opposite: The 15th-century mosque of Shaykh Ahmad ibn 'Alwan at Yafrus, a popular place of pilgrimage

in the east, Damt in the west and Juban in the south. Today Rada' is the seat of regional government, thriving on its position astride the route between north and south.

The commercial prosperity of the Rasulids had stemmed at least partly from their wide-ranging contacts all over the Islamic world. The Tahirids, home-grown as they were, perpetuated those contacts, investing their gains in fine buildings in Rada' and Juban, particularly under the last Tahirid sultan, 'Amir ibn 'Abd al-Wahhab (1489–1517). Of the two, Rada' remains the more interesting, partly because of that north-south road, a major smuggling route prior to unification. Its handsome stone houses are set in walled gardens and orchards, there is a flourishing market, and a citadel with the inevitable pre-Islamic foundations. 'Very fine and

A corner of the 15th-century 'Amiriyyah madrasah in Rada', built by the last Tahirid sultan, 'Amir ibn 'Abd al-Wahab

beautiful,' reported Ludovico de Varthema in his *Travels*, published in 1510, 'populous and rich.'[98] Varthema was a Bolognese merchant who was captured by the Tahirids in Aden (where he saw the Sultan reviewing an army of 80,000 men for an expedition against San'a and the Zaydi Imams) and imprisoned in great hardship for three months in Rada'. Pretending to be mad to save his life, de Varthema's whiteness incurred the passionate interest of the Sultan's wife. 'Would to God that this man was my husband,' de Varthema reported her as exclaiming. Despite his rejection of her advances he was finally released and able to travel round the country, his account of Yemen one of the earliest by a European.

The pride of Rada' is the 500-year old 'Amiriyyah madrasah, built to reinforce Sunni orthodoxy. It has recently been undergoing a major restoration. It is an excellent demonstration of how far-ranging, even in this seemingly remote town, those Tahirid contacts were. Influenced, inevitably, by the Rasulid buildings in Ta'izz, the 'Amiriyyah also brings together the many elements of indigenous Yemeni architecture that we have seen in other parts of the country, above all that passion for plastic and surface decoration. Crenellations, densely carved stucco dadoes, mihrab niche and walls and window embrasures in the prayer hall, painted decoration on the interior of domes, as festooned with stars as the pavilions of the Alhambra, make this one of the finest flourishes of Yemeni architecture. Only a visit or the book describing its restoration by Selma al-Radi can really do it justice.[99]

In Yemen, exposed to African, Indian, even Mediterranean influences, surface decoration has a distinctive panache that one sees even in the way people dress themselves. In Rada' even the local 'tablecloth' or *sitarah*, with which women cover

Painted interlacing decoration inside al-'Amariyyah madrasah, Rad'a

themselves, echoes the painted decoration of the 'Amiriyyah.

Early in the sixteenth century a new threat to Tahirid prosperity appeared – the Portuguese. A Portuguese vessel sailed into the Red Sea in 1504, with designs on Indian Ocean trade and control of the Red Sea and plans to harass the local shipping. Unfortunately for Sultan 'Amir, the Tahirid ruler at the time, the Portuguese intrusions attracted the attention of the Mamluk rulers of Egypt, as fearful for the security of their Red Sea trade as for the safety of Mecca and Madina. In 1516 the Mamluks carried their campaign against the Portuguese into Yemen, against the Tahirids but in alliance with the Zaydis, and defeating Sultan 'Amir in a confrontation outside San'a. He fled up Jabal Nuqum and on to the fortress of Dhu Marmar but was caught on the way up that precipitous cliff, decapitated and his head carried to San'a. Once again Yemen was in the hands of foreign rulers.[100]

VIII EXCURSIONS: HADHRAMAWT

From Rada' an ancient caravan track heads eastward, skirting the Ramlat Sab'atayn. Eventually, after several camel days, it reaches the desert fort of al-'Abr, a frontier garrison in British days and a major source of fresh water from which caravan trails radiate in all directions. The route from Rada' fell into disuse with the hardening of frontiers between the British and Marxists in the south and Ottomans, Imam and Republicans in the north, and became good only for smuggling. From Rada', heading northeast, it is only a few more camel days past ancient Shabwah to Shibam, medieval capital of Wadi Hadhramawt. This is the great valley which extends some 600 kilometres from its source in the desert near al-'Abr to its mouth at Sayhut on the Arabian Sea; in its lower reaches east of Tarim it changes its name to Wadi Masilah and becomes a perennial river, instead of a dry water course, flowing through an ever narrower defile.

Almost any approach to Wadi Hadhramawt is dramatic. One of the most sensational is from the air. The flight from San'a more or less follows the same route as that from Rada'. Suddenly the forbidding volcanic plateau known as the Jawl or Jol comes into view, the ruins of the great incense depot of Shabwah lost in the heat haze a little way to the south of the aircraft. The surface of the Jawl is carved by a thousand water courses that have eaten into its surface to form a jigsaw puzzle on the ground. Then a wide watercourse, far wider at its forty-kilometre entrance near al-'Abr than all the others, gradually narrows; the plane flies lower to reveal tiny oases either side of the wadi frugally watered by wells and by run-off from the plateau; and finally, if the pilot is obliging, the plane skims over the rooftops of Shibam and lands a minute later at Sayun.

To comprehend the isolation of the Wadi one should follow in the footsteps of some of its early European visitors – Theodore and Mabel Bent among the most intrepid in 1893, Harold Ingrams and his wife Doreen in 1934, Freya Stark in 1935. If you do this, there is an extraordinary moment when after trekking from the coast for many miles over the dreary and impoverished Jawl ('looking as if a giant coal scuttle had been upset,' wrote the Bents;[101] 'bare as a gridiron under the rays of sunlight', according to Freya Stark[102]), you are suddenly brought to a halt by the realisation that you are standing on the edge of one of those jigsaw faults; and when very cautiously you take one more step, you look three hundred metres down on the most unexpected and revitalising river of green, the date palms of Wadi Du'an or another of the wadis running from the south into

Opposite: *Shibam, Wadi Hadhramawt: aerial view of spotless rooftops surrounding the Great Mosque*

Qabr Hud, tomb of the pre-Islamic prophet in Wadi Masilah. The rock said to be Hud's petrified camel is just below the main shrine

the main Wadi Hadhramawt, with fortified mud villages clinging miraculously to the walls of the escarpment.

The name Hadhramawt is used both for the Wadi and for the wider region, including the coast at Mukalla and al-Shihr and also the tributary side wadis. Pre-history and history join almost continuously in Hadhramawt where a succession of archaeologists have dug into its cliffs to discover Palaeolithic and Neolithic remains, Bronze Age tail tombs and settlements, and first millennium temples (the Russians at Raybun, the Englishwoman Gertrude Caton Thompson at Huraydhah).[103] The caravans laden

with aromatics and spices avoided the Wadi, preferring to head inland from the sheltered harbour of Qana to Shabwah at its western end. The area was so famous from the incense trade that Pliny the Elder, in writing about Sabota/Shabwah, even mentions the honey of the region, which never crystallizes and is more costly than gold (the price today is still vast, and the local honey men turned up their noses when asked to try my crystallised honey from London). After the destruction of Shabwah at the end of the third century AD, probably by the Himyarites, Shibam became the leading city of Hadhramawt.

Local mythology presents a slightly different version, attributing the populating of Hadhramawt to 'Ad, a race of giants whose tombs, at least seven metres long, occur at various places in the Wadi, perhaps related to those tail tombs which archaeologists have dated to the second millennium BC. And then there is Genesis ('you cannot help it,' wrote Ingrams in *Arabia and the Isles*, 'in Hadhramaut you are living in Genesis'[104]), with Joktan alias Qahtan and his son Hazarmareth from whose name Hadhramawt (interpreted by some as meaning place or presence of death) is believed to derive; then the tribes of Kindah who invaded from the north before the coming of Islam, which is where we shall pick up the story.

Holy men have played an important role in Hadhramawt, the holiest being the Prophet Hud, whose tomb in Wadi Masilah attracts the largest annual ziyarah, lasting three days. Hud was reputed to be the great-great-grandson of Noah, who called his people to repentance until he was hunted down by his enemies and chased up against the cliff of the wadi where God opened the rock for him and he disappeared inside. His camel, poor creature, was left outside and remains, petrified, at the entrance, the huge boulder reminiscent of other holy Arabian stones such as the smaller Ka'bah in the Great Mosque in Mecca. As with the rest of Yemen, Hadhramawt made a rapid conversion to Islam at first, before suffering from the inevitable backsliding; but around 900 the Hadhramis were redeemed by Sayyid Ahmad ibn 'Isa al-Muhajir from Basra whose forceful preaching converted pagans and heretical Muslims alike. His much revered tomb is just east of Sayun. Often the *barakah* or blessing of the holy man encouraged others to want to be buried near him, as at the cemetery at 'Aynat or in Sayun's cemetery where the delicious turquoise dome of the tomb of Ahmad ibn Zayn al-Hibshi dominates those of lesser mortals at its feet. Visits to the tombs on special days – ziyarahs – are the occasion for processions, pilgrimages, markets, while the tombs are bedecked with rags and charms and stones, even the occasional animal's horn.

This may make Hadhramawt seem more spiritual than its history indicates. Two other factors have been rather more significant. Tribalism made it a perpetual battleground until a local Hadhrami philanthropist, whose wealth derived from property in Singapore, requested British help in the 1930s to establish peace; the Hadhrami was Sayyid Abubakr ibn Shaykh al-Kaf, the British official sent to assist was Harold Ingrams and the peace (funded largely by Sayyid Abubakr) became known as 'Ingrams' Peace'.[105] That state of warfare aggravated the other factor: the dearth of water. Limited water resources meant peace was essential for the control of rainwater and its direction to the limited cultivable land, and also for trade between coast and interior. When peace broke down migration, in the footsteps of generations of Hadhramis driven abroad by economic or political pressures, was the only solution – to East Africa, to Singapore, to Indonesia and in recent years to the oil-rich countries of Arabia, especially Saudi Arabia; some of the most successful Hadhramis in Saudi Arabia are the Bin Laden family.

Two tribes in particular have dominated Hadhrami life for the last four hundred years: Kathiri and Qu'aiti. The Kathiris are thought to have migrated to the Wadi in the fifteenth century. The extent of their authority varied and in the sixteenth century they summoned tribal mercenaries from Yafa' in the west to suppress local rebellions. This was a great mistake, for the Yafa'is soon challenged the Kathiris and established a separate state based at al-Qatn. They went on to develop an important connection with India, supplying mercenaries to the Nizam of Hyderabad. The leaders of these troops, the Qu'aiti clan, often married local women, and wealth acquired in India enabled them to extend their power in Hadhramawt, where their dominance was recognised by the British in 1888.

It was in answer to appeals from Kathiri notables that Ingrams was despatched in 1936 to see

Bee hives in Wadi Du'an; the local honey was known even to Pliny in the 1st century AD

Left: *Aerial view of Shibam, its houses tightly packed inside the walls in the middle of the wadi. A new suburb on the other side of the floodbed caters for population expansion*

Opposite: *A cool and shady street between high-rise mudbrick houses in Shibam*

if he could bring some kind of settlement to the area. Hadhramawt was effectively divided between these two tribal groups, with the Qu'aiti family eventually controlling the larger part of the Wadi including the town of Shibam, the Kathiris the small enclave round Sayun and Tarim. The Qu'aitis also controlled the ports of Mukalla and al-Shihr.

Migration produces a curious dichotomy in Hadhrami life: an outlook on the wider world encouraged by exchange of goods, news, investment and the tendency of migrants to return in old age and for the wealthier ones to build themselves exotic palaces, contrasted with extreme conservatism particularly in religious matters which are dominated by the sayyids, (descendants of the Prophet), concentrated in Tarim.[106] Because of the time needed to reach the Wadi, by whatever means, its isolation is what makes the strongest first impression. But other images soon crowd in: the intricate patterns woven by fields of cereals and

groves of date palms; the totally covered women working in the fields or returning at dusk, their tall pointed 'witch' hats bobbing on the donkey carts taking them home; the outlandish faces in Sayun suq; the acres of drying mud brick and the lime kilns producing lime plaster for the houses – clearly a lot of money is entering the area for new houses. And then there are the houses themselves: the seven-storey high-rise houses of Shibam, the vast palace of the Kathiri sultan in Sayun, the palatial fantasies of the al-Kaf family in Tarim.

It is mud architecture at its most superlative and breeze blocks are still easily outnumbered by mud bricks. The houses are always cool even in mid-summer and cunning variations in the decoration of the exterior provides contrasts of light and shade – such as the horizontal fluted decoration on the lower levels of Tarim houses – to ease the eye even at midday. Outward-sloping walls give light to upper floors, shade to the street. Stepped

pyramid or crow-step decoration on roof tops or over doorways is one of the oldest architectural decorations in the world, found all over Mesopotamia and Arabia. It is found even in Petra, introduced from north-west Arabia.[107]

The three main towns of Hadramawt – Shibam, Sayun and Tarim – are very different from each other. Shibam is the oldest of the three, 'the eye and backbone of Hadhramawt', the only town to have been built in the middle of the Wadi, on a mound that undoubtedly conceals older foundations. Its position has rendered it vulnerable to floods; one in 1982 led to a UNESCO survey and suggested conservation project, little of which has been carried out, however.[108] Shibam's distinctive architecture is designed for defence, for climatic comfort and social custom; it's a very particular sensation to be invited inside a house, to climb seemingly endless stairs and finally to collapse on cushions in a spacious and miraculously cool *majlis*. The town took over as administrative centre

from Shabwah around the fourth century AD and subsequently prospered from taxation of the caravan trade. None of the buildings dates from this early period although the main congregational mosque is said to have been repaired by a Ziyadid ruler in the tenth century. It was twice destroyed in the thirteenth and sixteenth centuries but has altered little since its last rebuilding in the late sixteenth century. A few of the houses may also be around four hundred years old but most are about a hundred. Mudbrick needs constant maintenance and this has been difficult since the nationalisation of housing in 1972 and control of rents. The advent of mains drainage has not helped either; poorly installed and maintained, it has created a rising water table which has severely undermined the foundations of many houses.

One enters the town through its main gate, a heterogeneous structure, neo-classical on the outside, oriental fantasy inside. Within the walls there were some five hundred houses, their number

Sayun: The towering mudbrick palace of the Kathiri sultans, built with part of the fortune the sultans made in Singapore in the early 20th century

*The turquoise-domed tomb
of Ahmad al-Hibshi
in Sayun cemetery*

limited by the town authorities; hence the development of a suburb on the far side of the wadi to take the overflow. The inconvenience of the seven-storey houses is mitigated by bridges between their upper floors, preserving privacy for women visiting neighbours and also sheer human energy. Even chickens are lowered to the ground in cages each morning to save owners the bother of taking them downstairs in person. Houses are entered through elaborately carved doors, locks released either from inside by a rope that can be pulled from an upper storey or from the outside by a curious wooden key that looks like a giant toothbrush. Within, space is strictly allocated to family, reception, preparation of food. The rooftop generally has a high parapet pierced by openings through which the street can be surveyed.

But social events such as weddings can take place in the street, which are cool and shady even at midday; we once stumbled on such a party, the whole town assembled to take part in the music and dancing.

Shibam was Qu'aiti territory but Sayun, east of Shibam, and Tarim, still further east, were Kathiri. Sayun is the most outward looking of the three towns; its little suq is full of foreign goods and the faces of the motorbike taxi drivers look as if they have just driven in from Java. The market square is dominated by the Sultan's palace, a marvel of mudbrick architecture, financed by Kathiri investments in Singapore. In nearby streets shops are filled with exotic fabrics and fantastic costumes; clearly behind the well-maintained but secretive walls of the houses life must be a constant round of parties. The town is divided, like all towns, into quarters, each marked by its whitewashed neighbourhood mosque surmounted by a stubby white minaret; entrances are often elaborated with crenellations and carved decoration. The cemetery mentioned above is central, dominated by the turquoise-roofed dome of the al-Hibshi tomb. 'Why is turquoise such a common colour in the Islamic world?' is a regular question; the answer must surely be that since so much of that world

The 50-metre-high mudbrick minaret of the al-Mihdar mosque in Tarim; it is the tallest minaret in south Arabia

is arid and monotonous, nowhere more so than the ominous volcanic wastes of the Jawl, turquoise symbolises water, the waters of Paradise so revered by all Muslims, as indeed in the garden villas of the Kathiris on the edge of their bustling metropolis.

Eastwards and on the other side of the Wadi is Tarim, the religious centre of Hadhramawt and main base of the sayyids, a seat of religious learning with a famous library of medieval manuscripts and Qurans attached to the congregational mosque. The most striking mosque, however, is al-Mihdar, originally dating from the fifteenth century but completely rebuilt in 1914, its fifty-metre high minaret like a beacon welcoming the

stranger when glimpsed across the Wadi. So orthodox were the sayyids, the religious aristocracy of Hadhramawt and mainstay of the Kathiris, that some of them would not even look at Freya Stark, a woman and a non-Muslim – horrors! – and she was certainly not allowed inside the celebrated library. She found her compensation, however, in an al-Kaf garden (full of bougainvillea, pools and sunbirds): 'we would sit on a carpet in a garden, with pomegranates in flower … and talk of history, or religion, the ancient borders of Hadhramawt, or the policy of the League of Nations, with the agreeable feeling that these matters were all about equally distant from our repose.'[109] Harold Ingrams captured another aspect: arriving in Tarim after a long and exhausting journey from Sayun (now about one and a half hours by car) he was welcomed by a group of al-Kaf milllionaires at the entrance to one of their grander palaces and in due course was shown to his room and bathroom equipped with a marble bath, a basin with *running* water, a shower, snow-white towels, 'and wonder of wonders a real "pull and let go", an item scarcely to be seen even in Aden. What was even more wonderful was that *everything* worked–!'[110]

Tarim has suffered perhaps even more than Shibam from nationalisation and sequestration, the upkeep of the palaces dependent on remittances from abroad and tender loving care which members of the al-Kaf family can no longer afford. It remains to be seen whether the greater security of unification will encourage private conservation measures since the government can also ill afford them. Money has certainly begun to flow back into the Wadi, demonstrated by the quantities of mud bricks laid out to dry. Construction has always been viewed in the Middle East as the safest form of investment; now Yemenis need to look at conservation as well.

Once again one has to wander among the fields, the canals, the date groves to come to grips with the continuity of this part of the world. A huge canal not far from Tarim has been lined for ever by thick groves of trees, a haven for migrating birds including grey herons motionless on one leg beside its well-stocked waters. Walking where Sayun fades into the countryside, one might see an old man kneading lime with which to white-wash walls, a pump (dread sound in a region of depleting aquifers) gushing water into narrow channels to wash the feet of date palms. Or making the hackneyed climb above the suburbs of Shibam, one catches the sunset over the Jawl, much as those incense-carrying caravans must have seen it on their long trek northwards with their precious loads.

Down on the Hadhrami coast dhows from Somalia, from Djibouti and Eritrea, bigger boats from the Malabar coast of India, little fishing boats from other fishing villages bob up and down in the harbours of Mukalla and al-Shihr.[111] They are not ideal shelters, and had to be rejected when it came to choosing a coaling station for steamers of the East India Company in the 1830s.[112] But in the fish bars and teashops adjoining Mukalla harbour there is a healthy flavour of the Indian Ocean – Arabs, Indians, Africans rubbing shoulders or shouting abuse as they did in the days of

The port of Mukalla: watercolour c. 1830 by Robert Moresby, painted while he was looking for suitable coaling stations for the new steamships (Searight Collection, Victoria & Albert Museum)

the *Periplus of the Erythraean Sea*.[113] Beyond al-Shihr the surfaced road continues another 280 kilometres as far as Sayhut where the Ingramses emerged via Wadi Masilah from their first visit to Hadhramawt in 1934. Since the 1990s an oil company has dented the isolation, its production (around 200,000 barrels a day in 1999) easing Yemen's sad imbalance of payments.

The Ingramses' journey down Wadi Masilah had taken them some of the way into Mahrah country – 'row on row of mountains, each higher than the last, till they were hidden among the clouds,' wrote Ingrams.[114] It is a little known part of the country whose tribal dialects (known as Modern South Arabian) may prove to be linked with the people occupying southern Arabia prior to the Semitic infiltrations at the end of the second millennium BC. Some Mahri tribes claim to be descendants of the Himyarites.

In language and custom they are closely linked with other tribes in the mountains of Dhofar in Oman and in Soqotra; indeed the leading personality of the area was the Sultan of Qishn (on the Mahrah coast) and Soqotra, the latter colonised from the Mahrah in the tenth century. Tribes are intensely jealous of their territories: 'going into Mahrah country,' Ingrams noted, 'reminded me of travelling in an international train where the

Tribesman overlooking the Mahrah wilderness

nationalities of the ticket collectors change at every frontier.'[115] The tribes were mainly nomadic and bred camels apparently famous for their speed and for working at night; a British official, Philip Allfree visiting the area in the 1940s on horseback found people in the Mahrah who had never seen horses. The camel owners were even more famous for their fractiousness, brilliantly described by Allfree, who had the mixed blessing of working in their midst in the 1960s.[116]

When it comes to describing this haunting part of the world Freya Stark is irresistible. 'I was reading *Morte d'Arthur* at the time,' she writes about her visit to Wadi Du'an (did she really carry it with her?), 'and found it harmonised strangely with the life of the wadi: its sudden contrasts, the splendour of its castles, the general uncertainty of things around them, the delightful feeling that anything might happen anywhere and not be surprising. The average inhabitant of Hadhramaut takes much the same view of life as Malory's knights on the marches of Cornwall or Wales: a stranger under a tree has the same lively possibilities in him – a suitable object for either a fight or a feast; and the fifteenth century ideas of convalescence in England' – she was sick at the time – 'must have been very much the same as those in

Women returning home from the fields near Shibam; each area in Wadi Hadhramawt has its own style of hat, but all are tall

Arabia now, where you are expected to rise from your bed ready for anything as Sir Tristram, lying ill, was badgered to joust by his friends.'[117]

IX INCURSIONS: ADEN AND THE RED SEA

In 1504 a Portuguese caravel sailed boldly through the narrow straits of Bab al-Mandab into the Red Sea, challenging the Muslim monopoly of this major link between the Mediterranean and the Indian Ocean. Not only that: this Christian incursion was viewed as a direct threat to the security of the holy places of Islam – Mecca and Madina. In Muslim eyes the Red Sea deserved the same respect as other hajj routes across Arabia, the Levant and northern Africa, so that the Portuguese incursion was seen as a religious as well as a commercial threat.[118]

The story of Yemen between the sixteenth and mid-twentieth centuries is woven inextricably into a pattern of European incursions and Muslim reactions. Concern for their trade led the Mamluk rulers of Egypt to Yemen to exclude the Portuguese, and the same policy was subsequently adopted by the Ottoman Turks, who intermittently absorbed Yemen into their Empire for three hundred and fifty years. The Ottomans were effectively chased out by a revived Zaydi Imamate in the 1630s, but returned in the late nineteenth century as a reaction to the spread of European imperialism – notably the British in Aden – and the internationalisation of the Red Sea following the opening of the Suez Canal. Again the Imamate rallied successfully in the north against the intruder but in the south the British protected their position with a network of tribal relationships, developing

Opposite: Reading the Quran in the mosque of Sayyid Abdullah al-Aidarus, in Crater, Aden

Right: Somali goats on offer in Aden, brought over from the Horn of Africa

A photograph (c.1900) of the Aden tanks, built in the early centuries AD to collect and store rainwater

into the protectorates of the mid-twentieth century.

Aden was the first to feel the impact of the Portuguese incursion. It occupies a magnificent site on a peninsula formed by the crater of an extinct volcano, about a hundred nautical miles from the mouth of the Red Sea. The main town, today known as Crater, now joined to the mainland by the sandy neck of Khormaksar, had already developed by the first millennium BC. Crater is still the cosmopolitan heart of Aden and, even as Evelyn Waugh wrote in the 1930s, the smells are unchanged – 'spices, woodsmoke, incense, goats, delicious Arab and Indian kitchen smells, garlic and curry, sewage and hair oil.'[119]

To the west the five hundred-metre Jabal Shamshan towers above the town, The minimal rainfall which it attracted was carefully stored in the series of tanks, excavated and constructed probably in the Himyarite period, that spill down the sides of the mountain, some thirteen in all, once capable of holding around two million litres of water. A gap in the mountain range known as North Pass leads to the nineteenth and twentieth century administrative centre of Aden: coming through the pass one looks out over Back Bay and Steamer Point, once filled with steamers from around the world, stacking their holds with coal before steaming up the Red Sea or out into the Indian Ocean. Shipping fell away during the years of the socialist republic but there are ambitious plans for its revival. The lip of the wider crater continues across a causeway – pink flamingoes to left and right – to the once raunchy suburb of Shaykh Uthman, in Waugh's day the alleged brothel of Aden, and seedbed of the industrial troubles that erupted in the 1950s and 1960s. The crater is finally rounded off at Little Aden, which the present Adeni authorities are remodelling to be the nucleus of the revived international port.

Aden's prosperity rose and fell with the fortunes of the kingdoms and governments of the interior of this corner of Arabia. It was known as Eudaemon Arabia to the Greeks, as Arabia Emporium to the Romans. Tribal troubles around the beginning of the Christian era upset Aden's trade so that the first century AD mariners' guide to the area – the *Periplus of the Erythraean Sea* – reckoned that Aden had seen better days.[120] A century later its prosperity revived with the arrival of Roman ships in the Indian Ocean, around 150–60 AD, aromatics and spices its raison d'être (the town was famous for its dealers in these commodities even in the 1870s when over six hundred tons of incense were handled by Adeni merchants). Firm government under Islamic dynasties such as the thirteenth to fifteenth century Rasulids and fifteenth to sixteenth century Tahirids gave Adeni merchants the security essential to commercial ventures that could then take full advantage of the sheltered harbour, sweet water and seasonal winds. Marco Polo at the end of the thirteenth century commented on the wealth of its Sultan (probably the Rasulid al-Muzaffar) as one of the richest princes in the world, who could allegedly send an army of 30,000 horsemen and 40,000 infantry to campaign in Syria, his wealth deriving from taxes on merchandise passing through Aden. He also pointed out the advantages of Aden's 'excellent port' filled with vessels arriving from India with spices and drugs, transhipped in Aden to smaller vessels for the voyage up the Red Sea to Egypt.[121]

Aden's significance was immediately appreciated by the Portuguese when they set out early in the sixteenth century to control the rich traffic of the Indian Ocean. 'This place has a greater and richer trade than any other in the world,' wrote the Portuguese historian Duarte Barbosa, 'and also this trade is in the most valuable commodities.'[122] Most important in Portuguese eyes it guarded the entrance to the Red Sea, ensuring that east-west trade was conducted via Egypt (Alexandria) and the Mediterranean (Venice). When that first Portuguese vessel entered the Red Sea in 1504 it was aiming to cut the throat of that trade, redirecting it via the newly discovered Cape route. In

An aerial view c.1940 of the western end of the Aden peninsula, looking down on Steamer Point and Post Office in the right foreground, the Crescent in the middle and Maala behind

1506 the Portuguese built a small fort on Soqo-tra and in 1513 their admiral Alfonso de Albuquerque was directed to lay siege to Aden.[123] Albuquerque's siege failed partly because of defective scaling ladders, but mainly because of the admiral's underestimation of Aden's strength; ten years earlier de Varthema had commended Aden as 'the strongest city that was ever seen on level ground', a curious comment considering how unlevel the ground actually is.[124] Its medieval fortifications have largely disappeared, but in their time they had kept the Portuguese at bay and indeed nearly the Ottomans too, who only captured the settlement in 1538 after a long and bitter siege.

This Portuguese intrusion into the Red Sea brought them close enough to Mecca to alert the Mamluk rulers of Egypt, supposed guardians of the holy places, who in 1516 despatched an expedition to drive the Portuguese from the Red Sea. Almost by accident they found themselves invited into Yemen by tribes opposing the Tahirids. A year later, however, the Mamluks were themselves defeated in both Syria and Egypt by the Ottomans who in due course – in 1538 – claimed the guardianship for themselves, including Yemen and its main port, Aden. The locals tried to throw the Ottomans out in 1547, even appealing to the Portuguese for help, though without success.

Ottoman occupation of the whole country, working up to Ta'izz from Aden and to San'a direct from Tihamah, took nearly ten years; it was never secure and its main achievement was the creation of a cohesive Imamate opposition. Nevertheless the Turks put up some fine buildings in San'a, including the Bakiriyyah mosque near the citadel, modelled on contemporary mosques in Constantinople.

Opposition to the Ottomans rallied gradually around the Zaydi Imams, whose harrying persuaded the Ottomans to cut their losses and in 1635 to hand over the country to the Imamate, with San'a as its capital until Imam Ahmad shifted it to Ta'izz after 1948. The country remained technically part of the Ottoman Empire, however, as did the whole Arabian shore of the Red Sea. Zaydi control of the southern areas of the

Aden harbour (formerly Back Bay), sheltered from the winds of the Indian Ocean, seen from Crater Pass

Offices of the Peninsular & Orient Company (P&O), developers of steam trade between India and Britain, with HMS Glasgow and HMS Wolverine in harbour (photograph c.1880)

country was always insecure, with parts breaking away to establish local autonomy. This was the case, for instance, with Lahij whose Sultan declared his independence of Zaydi rule in the eighteenth century, thereby facilitating a later alien intrusion.

From the seventeenth century to the early nineteenth European incursions were limited to their coffee dealings. So popular did coffee drinking become in Europe that the pirate John Avery (who briefly occupied the island of Perim at the mouth of the Red Sea assuming it to be a well-placed jumping-off ground for his attack on trading vessels until he discovered it was waterless) complained of his colleagues abandoning piracy in favour of coffee trading. In 1798, however, occurred an event which upset Red Sea relationships far more drastically than incursions by Portuguese or pirates. Napoleon invaded Egypt that year, with a view to cutting British communications with India via the Red Sea, a route increasingly advocated by merchants frustrated by the length of the Cape route. The British, aghast at the prospect of French control of the Egyptian route, despatched an expedition from India which camped briefly on Perim on its way up the Red Sea, but so slow were communications with India that the French had already been defeated before the British expedition even reached

Ship passengers relaxing in an Aden hotel. From Harry Furniss, Sketches in Pen and Ink, *c.1897 (courtesy P&O)*

the Nile. British merchants had already eyed the Red Sea as a faster alternative to the Cape route to India, a British visitor in 1804 commenting that Aden was the only good port in Arabia Felix and 'has the great advantage over every harbour, within the straits, that it can be quitted at all seasons.' 'The Gibraltar of the East,' one visitor, Lord Valentia, called it.[125]

Aden's geographical location became an even greater strength when technology gave vessels on the open sea the power to outwit the monsoon. In 1831 the East India Company in Bombay launched the paddle steamer *Hugh Lindsay*. She was to steam from Bombay to Suez to meet mail and passengers sent overland from Alexandria, where they had arrived by steam from Falmouth (later Southampton). This was 'the harbinger of future vessels,' rhapsodised a Bombay newspaper, 'who will waft us to our native shores with speed and pleasure.'[126] Not much pleasure on the maiden voyage from Bombay to Suez and back, however; the little vessel was insufficiently powered, even with coal piled up on the decks and in the cabins. Extra coal had been deposited at Aden thanks to its overlord the Sultan of Lahij; Aden, at that time, because of the shift to Mokha, had declined to 'a desolate, straggling village with barely a thousand inhabitants' (and 'a few minarets tottering to their fall' said Wellsted, discoverer of that first South Arabian inscription at Husn al-Ghurab, the great rock that towers over Qana, along the coast).[127]

In 1837 the East India Company offered to buy Aden from the Sultan of Lahij, who suggested an annual rent but ultimately spurned the deal. The same year, however, an Indian vessel, the *Duria Dawlah*, was raided off Aden and its pilgrim passengers manhandled. This was just the pretext the Bombay government needed and in 1839 Captain Haines of the Indian Navy was despatched to occupy the peninsula.

Haines' task was not difficult; it took the small expeditionary force only a few hours to capture the town, although from Haines' point of view it turned out to be a thankless task. British occupation established a relatively peaceful haven in a turbulent region but the garrison remained in a state of semi-siege from hostile Yemeni neighbours for several years, necessitating funds from the East India Company in Bombay which it was always reluctant to pay. The Bombay government was only interested in Aden as a coal depot, in the Red Sea as a highway, and wanted no greater involvement.[128]

Governments might be mean but merchants were quick to seize on Aden's revived potential as an Indian Ocean emporium, especially after the inauguration of the Suez Canal in 1869. Within a few months French, Austrian, Dutch vessels were calling at Aden to refuel with coal, determined to ensure the Red Sea remained an international waterway. The British in Aden, in India and in London looked askance at such assumptions and from a simple way station Aden rapidly developed into a lynchpin of British naval imperialism.

Prosperity followed imperialism; Aden once again became the great emporium of the Indian Ocean, the settlement's new prosperity largely developed by Bombay Indians – craftsmen and builders as well as the soberly dressed father figures of the tightly-knit Parsee community. The latter used every opportunity not only to corner the coast trade but also to extend other forms of trade throughout the area. Ever larger vessels resulted in the abandonment of Aden's Front Bay, facing the breezes of the Indian Ocean, for the Back Bay, dredged deeper in the 1880s and more sheltered for the bunkering on which Aden was to thrive.

'What a scene of desolation and dreariness Aden presents to the newcomer! and how soon one gets to like the place in spite of it all.' So wrote the traveller Walter Harris in 1893 at the start of his *Journey through the Yemen*.[129] Generations of Cowasjees and Muncherjees sent boats out to the steamers to enquire after passengers' needs and satisfy them at their well-stocked emporia on Prince of Wales Crescent. Occasionally passengers had the luxury of a night ashore – staggering on their sea legs to carriages that whisked them across the narrow isthmus to the town situated in the sun-scorched crater, or along the blown, blistered Esplanade to the Crescent Hotel overlooking the dusty but indubitably imperial parade ground of Aden's garrison.

It was partly these European encroachments on what was still regarded as an Ottoman preserve, but also in response to growing anarchy in the central highlands and Tihamah, that led to the Ottoman re-occupation of Yemen from 1849, when an Ottoman force landed in Hodeida. The landing had little effect on the chaos in the highlands, but with the opening of the Suez Canal it was easier to move troops to Yemen and in 1871 the Ottomans moved up into the highlands to reoccupy San'a. Although in due course the Ottomans brought tranquillity to certain parts of the country, a British commentator, G. Wyman Bury, visiting Yemen in the early 1900s, wrote woefully in his *Arabia Infelix* that 'the happiness of this country has seldom been noticeable and its woes have waxed with the ripening years until they bid fair to culminate in a crop which the sword alone can harvest.'[130]

Ottoman and British were bound to clash over control of this cornerstone of their imperial policies (and almost immediately did so, in 1873, over control of Lahij north of Aden) but from the 1890s the Ottomans were obliged to some extent to accommodate the British as their regime came under ferocious attack from a new dynamic Imam, Muhammad ibn Yahya Hamid al-Din. In 1904 Muhammad was succeeded by his son Yahya, the dominant figure in Yemeni politics for the next forty years. Initiating a national liberation movement, Imam Yahya almost immediately besieged San'a with around 15,000 tribal followers. Garrisons in Hajjah and Yarim surrendered to him. By 1911 the two sides came to an agreement, the Imam controlling the highlands, the Ottomans Tihamah.

Meanwhile, in the years immediately before World War I, British authorities in the south and Ottoman Turkish authorities in the north accepted a frontier between their two spheres of influence, effectively dividing Yemen into north and south. The division, part of the carve-up of the Ottoman Empire, was never recognised by the Zaydi Imams, least of all Imam Yahya who assumed control of the north with the abolition of the Ottoman Empire at the end of the War, and dedicated himself to the reunification of his country.

A rugged inaccessible hinterland lay across the divide between the independent north and the British south. 'A chaos of grim, savage mountains,' wrote the botanist Hugh Scott, that rise to well over seven hundred metres. Wadi bottoms are shaded by tall-stemmed aloes, huge wild figs and stately *'ilb* trees, while the barren hillsides are occasionally enlivened by the hideous bloated stems of *Adenium obesum* and cactus-like euphorbias: 'A chaos of wild ranges cultivating chaos,' was another of Scott's comments – a state of affairs which the British authorities endeavoured to control in order to safeguard their vital imperial stronghold of Aden from tribal incursions from the north, encouraged by the Imam.[131]

This hinterland was a jigsaw puzzle of mini-states that lived in a state of almost chronic hostility towards each other, the inhabitants seemingly beyond authority, their loyalty often a question of who could supply the most rifles. British attempts to control them, described so graphically by Wyman Bury in *Land of Uz* and by the Master of Belhaven in his *Kingdom of Melchior*, seldom succeeded for long but Imam Yahya's efforts to entice them within his domain were also short-lived. The government in India had told Haines in 1839 that they would only retain Aden for the purpose of protecting a depot of coal, not for that of promoting intervention in the affairs of the neighbouring chiefs. But Haines, and even more his successors, found it essential to deal with the local tribes in order to ensure the safety of Aden.

British relations with the neighbours therefore began on a tentative and rudimentary basis but gradually took on a bigger role, buttressed with subsidies, arbitration, frontier settlements, and ultimately Treaties of Protection. Along the southwest corner of the peninsula and its immediate hinterland these were in place before World War I and the term 'Aden Protectorate' grew into common use after the delimitation of the frontier

Palace of the Sultan of Lahij in Lahij, the richest and most powerful of the frequently warring states of the Western Aden Protectorate; the Sultan also had a palace in Aden, now a museum

between British and Ottoman zones of influence. But it had no formal or constitutional existence until 1937 when responsibility for Aden passed from India to the Colonial Office and Aden became a Crown Colony. Following the establishment of Ingrams' Peace and a British advisory presence in Mukalla, the hinterland was divided for administrative purposes into Western and Eastern Aden Protectorates, the latter comprising Hadramawt and the Mahrah/Soqotra.

In fact the Imam's attention was distracted in the early 1930s by incursions from the north of his territory – from 'Asir, in what is now Saudi Arabia. In 1934, after battling with northern tribes led to

war with the newly formed and expansionist Saudi Arabia, Yahya negotiated a frontier agreement treaty with Saudi Arabia. Relations with Yemen's powerful northern neighbour have never been comfortable, but were expected to improve after a further agreement was signed in 2000.

Not surprisingly perhaps Yahya was determined his territory should be kept free of the ever expanding foreign grasp which he saw all round him. 'The Imam greatly fears any agreement with foreigners,' reported a Syrian visitor in the 1920s quoted by Robert Stookey, 'because such an agreement would one day provide an excuse for foreigners to interfere in the affairs of Yemen.'[132] But slowly the

country moved into the twentieth century: a few schools, hospitals (foreign doctors the only category of foreigners that was welcome), motor cars and bicycles, an airfield. There was a tendency among European visitors to mock Yahya's involvement in even the most minute of decisions, but others reported the rapport he built up with San'anis as well as in general with the tribesmen whose loyalty was both crucial and needing constant attention. The Imamate (as today's Presidency to a lesser extent) was dependent on the 'brute strength' of the tribes but had to be on constant alert against the primacy of tribal tradition over public order. Popular frustration at the slow pace of progress – in country as well as town – was behind Yahya's assassination in 1948, the apparent treachery of the tribes behind his successor Ahmad's decision to shift the capital and administration from San'a to Ta'izz, shuffling between his uncomfortable château there and the hot springs of 'Ayn al-Sukhna on the edge of Tihamah.

Internal opposition to northern and southern regimes developed from the mid-1950s, stimulated by the Suez fiasco and Egyptian President Nasser's vigorous anti-imperialist, pan-Arab propaganda. The port of Aden proved a focus for resentment either side of the north-south division, attracting northerners looking for employment, wider horizons, and education and locals resentful of British patronage of conservative tribal shaykhs. The death of Imam Ahmad in Ta'izz in 1962 triggered the military-led coup d'état in northern Yemen and the establishment of the Yemen Arab Republic in the north in the course of a bitter civil war (with the Egyptians coming in on the side of the republicans). In the south the British tried to contain nationalist agitation with the establishment of a Federation, uniting the conservative and backward shaykhdoms and sultanates of the Western Aden Protectorate with cosmopolitan and prosperous Aden, against a background of growing domestic and international pressures to quit. Increasing political violence spearheaded by the National Liberation Front (NLF) led to the collapse of the British-backed Federation in 1967, the handover of power to the NLF and the emergence of the socialist People's Democratic Republic of South Yemen (PDRY).[133]

Opposite: *Bugler of the Aden Protectorate Levies, 1940*

X THE SOQOTRA ARCHIPELAGO
Miranda Morris

Hundreds of millions of years ago, as geological epochs came and went, these small islands in the Indian Ocean witnessed the rise and fall of the continents of Asia and Africa on either side. Of all areas of Yemen, Soqotra has the richest and most ancient mythology – here, it is said, came the Sumerian hero Gilgamesh in the third millennium BC, in a bid to learn the secret of eternal life; the ancient Egyptians and Greeks had their own legends. Reality is as strange and beautiful as the legends – isolated from the world, plants and animals evolved into individual species which still flourish, looking (as they are) like left-overs from a primeval world.

The archipelago lies in the Gulf of Aden, a short detour from the main sea routes that crisscross the Indian Ocean, linking the Red Sea, India, Arabia and East Africa. It consists of four islands. The largest, Soqotra, lies some 380 kilometres south of Ras Fartak on the Arabian mainland; the second largest, the arid Abd al-Kuri, is some 80 kilometres off Cape Guardafui, and two smaller islands, Samha and the barren rock of Darsa are off the coast of Abd al-Kuri. Nearby rocks (locally called Saboniyat, in Arabic Siyal or Qaʻal Firʻawn) are important breeding sites for sea birds, attracted as are local fishermen by the rich surrounding waters. The total population of the archipelago is around 50,000, subsisting mainly on fishing and pasture. All three of the smaller islands are completely cut off from the outside world during the summer monsoon.

The administrative centre of the archipelago is on Soqotra itself at Hadiboh, home of the only electricity supply (other than private generators) and the only telephone. Most boats put in at the other main town, Qalansiyah, on the western

Opposite: A fisherman at Qalansiya casting his net in the shallow offshore waters. Only net and line fishing are possible for the five months of the summer monsoon when high winds keep the boats on shore
Below: A sheltered creek at Hadiboh on Soqotra, with the high granite Haggeher mountains behind

coastal plain, or ride just off Hadiboh, cargo and passengers being ferried to the shore in smaller boats. A small jetty has now been built east of Hadiboh, at Howlef – a sheltered bay long used by the dhow trade during the north-east monsoons.

The coastal plain which surrounds the island is broken from time to time by rocky headlands and limestone cliffs as well as by occasional date gardens. From the plain one climbs to the limestone plateau of the interior, intersected by deep ravines, cliffs and gullies which flow during a good rainy season and quickly become raging torrents after the periodic rain storms. But there is little permanent water on the plateau and it is only grazed after a good rainy season. It is dominated by the needle-like granite pinnacles of the 1,500-metre Haggeher mountains, well watered and usually cloud covered, crisscrossed by footpaths and animal tracks. Private grazing areas are enclosed by stone walls.

The archipelago was once part of the Gondwanaland super-continent but became isolated from Africa, Arabia and India when they separated in the Cretaceous period, at least sixty million years ago. It is part of the major tectonic plate of continental Africa, the deep Gulf of Aden carrying the main ever-widening fault that separates the Arabian and African plates. Its isolation explains the diversity and uniqueness of the Soqotran flora and fauna and also explains the legends which have enveloped the archipelago from the earliest times. Of the nine hundred or so plant species in the

Rising to 1,500 metres, the central Haggeher mountains of Soqotra catch the clouds that provide the island with much of its water

archipelago, over a third are endemic, unique to the archipelago, many of them remnants of ancient flora which long ago disappeared from the African-Asian mainland. The central mountains of Soqotra alone contain over two hundred endemic species.

The monsoon dominates the climate of the archipelago, effectively closing it to sea traffic and fishing from May to September. The salt-laden air and salty deposits on the pastureland (before the days of readily accessible salt, the islanders even used twigs dipped into the cooking pot in place of salt) make the livestock excessively thirsty, thereby imposing an extra burden on their herders who find it increasingly hard to find water for them as the water holes dry up. The winds of the north-east monsoon, which runs from November to March, are much milder and bring the precious winter rains but also winter storms. The transitional period between the two monsoons (end of March to early May) in most years brings the even more valuable gentle summer rains to some part of the island, though otherwise this is the hottest time of the year.

The vegetation watered by the monsoon has always been absolutely central to the lives of the majority of Soqotrans. Livestock rearing may for some be supplemented by date cultivation or by seasonal fishing, by periods spent working on the mainland as unskilled labour to earn hard cash or by cash input from a wage-earning member of the family, but it is rare to find a Soqotran family without livestock of any sort. Sheep, goats, camels, cattle and donkeys are supported solely by the island's vegetation.

As well as fodder for livestock, plants provide the basics of heat, light, fuel and building materials, as well as shade from the heat of the sun and shelter from wind and rain. Plants are even the source of fire: the skill of rubbing two sticks

A baby slung in a hammock suspended from the roof beams: the Soqotran cradle

together to produce a flame is still one possessed by most adult men and women on the islands. The ingenuity of the islanders enables them to produce all sorts of necessities from the vegetation that grows around them: medicines for people and livestock, glues, tinders, fertilisers, insecticides, cordage, pack saddles, house goods (mats, pots, baskets, containers), trade items, material for caulking boats, and even tubing for extracting scarce water from deep holes. Plant material is also used for less essential matters: for cosmetics and toys, for incense mixtures to perfume and fumigate the living quarters and clothing, and for pipes in which to smoke the powerful local tobacco.

Curiously shaped endemic Dracaena cinnabari *trees, source of a dark red resin known as cinnabar, or dragon's blood*

Nothing is wasted: even dead wood is put to use – layered with coral it goes into lime pits to make quicklime which is sold to the people of the more settled coastal villages to paint and waterproof their mosques and houses of mud and coral rag.

Of all the plants in the archipelago, perhaps the most famous is the endemic and unique *Dracaena*

cinnabari, the dragon's blood tree, a relic of Tertiary vegetation and the source of a resin used in lacquers and varnishes – reputedly even the varnish Stradivarius used for his violins. These trees are found in the highest parts of the island which catch the mists and damp of both the monsoons, but they grow especially thickly in the area called Rokeb di

Firmihin. The fruit of the tree is an important dry season fodder for the island livestock, the fresh leaves are good for making ropes and the dead leaves for bedding material. Even the dead tree has its uses: the trunk is made into drums, the branches into effective gutters and the friable core of the dead wood is stored as a tinder.

Probably the second most famous Soqotran plant is the Soqotran aloe which grows mainly in the high, dry areas at the western end of the island. Serjeant mentions that Soqotran aloes feature in trading lists at Marseilles in 1227, Florence in 1310–40 (but probably also before this) and again in a list of imports at Ragusa in 1458.[134] On the island the plant is of little importance in local usage, but there is still a steady demand for the dried juice which continues to be collected and dried in leather skins in the traditional manner in the hotter months.

Those indefatiguable travellers Theodore and Mabel Bent were greatly struck by other plants on Soqotra: 'the gouty, swollen-stemmed Adenium… the ugliest tree in creation, with one of the most beautiful flowers: it looks like one of the first efforts of Dame Nature in tree-making, happily abandoned by her for more graceful shapes and forms.'[135] Islanders are more appreciative of this tree: strips of the bark are cut off and tied around the necks of young kids and lambs to deter predatory ravens and wild cats, and its poisonous sap is rubbed into painful joints. 'Then there is the cucumber-tree, another hideous-stemmed tree, swollen and whitish; and the hill-slopes covered with these look as if they had been decorated with so many huge composite candles which had guttered horribly.'[136] The soft heartwood of these trees is chopped up and fed to goats if there is a serious drought. Frankincense trees, tree euphorbias, wild pomegranates, wild citrus were also spotted

Dendrosicyos socotrana, *or cucumber tree, described by the* Bents *as resembling a candle 'which had guttered horribly'. Its small fruits are inedible*

by the Bents. Problem plants include grass thorns that invade every garment, 'irritating to both body and mind', and the widespread species of Hibiscus whose leaves are covered in the finest of hairs which are extremely difficult to get out of the skin if one brushes against them.

Various plant products are offered for sale in the market in Hadiboh: the fruit of *Ziziphus spina-christi* used as food and its dried and pulverised leaves as cleansing material and medicine; tamarind pods; Euclea roots for cosmetic use; roots of

Salvadora persica for oral hygiene; the fresh resin of *Dracaena cinnabari* as medicine; the gum of various frankincense species; the dead wood of certain species which are appreciated for their smell when burned; dried aloe juice; certain lichens for which there is a demand on the mainland; *Aerva* flowering heads for stuffing bolsters and pillows, and honey. There is no tradition of bee-keeping on the island, but there are many honey hunters, and the Soqotra wild honey commands a high price, both on and off the island. It must be unique in the world, being produced as it is from the flowers of plants which grow nowhere else.

Perhaps the most striking aspect of the islands' fauna is the absence of predatory wild animals: there are no foxes, wolves or leopards, and not a single dog. The livestock of the archipelago are at risk only from wild and feral cats (that do at least keep the rats in check) or from the ravens that circle the skies continuously on the lookout for weak animals. Whereas on the mainland animals must be attended all day, on Soqotra they can be left to graze freely for weeks on end. Indeed in the highlands feral goats (and on the island of Samha even feral sheep) are a useful store of food for the hungriest years. Civet cats, thought to have been introduced to the island, used to be trapped, milked of a substance from anal glands used in the perfume industry, and then released.

Amongst the fauna of the archipelago birds are almost as specialised as the flora, with six endemic species among the two hundred species so far identified. Many birds were regarded even recently as a valuable food source: nesting seabirds, and especially their plump young, were caught on

Frankincense woodland in the Homhil valley on Soqotra. The frankincense produced by the many species of Boswellia of Soqotra was never as prized as that of the Boswellia sacra, *of the south Arabian mainland*

*Euphorbia abdelkuri which grows
only on Abd al-Kuri island*

daring night-time raids when the hunters were lowered over cliff edges on ropes; other land birds were caught in baited traps, or by using the latex of certain plants to make a bird lime which was dabbed around the water pools where the unfortunate birds came to drink at noon. The most visible bird of Soqotra is the Egyptian vulture: Soqotra has the biggest population of these birds anywhere in the Middle East, and it is highly regarded as scavenger. Other vertebrates include several species of bat much appreciated by the women who crawl into their caves to dig up the guano for use as fertiliser on their small garden plots.

Amongst the invertebrates there are about a hundred species of mollusc on the archipelago (terrestrial and freshwater), almost all endemic. All five scorpion species, a third of the 191 species of butterfly and moth, as well as other insect species are endemic. There are no poisonous snakes on the islands, and the only potentially harmful creature is the black widow spider although a giant centipede and a wolf spider have nasty bites. The

islanders are fond of the geckoes, skinks and lizards, but are fearful of the large Hemidactylus which they say will never let go once it has got its teeth into you, and keep a respectful distance from the chameleon, which is believed to make your voice go hoarse if it hisses in your face.

It is a surprise – a shock if you are paddling – to meet so many bright red and blue water crabs far inland and even high in the Haggeher mountains. There are also large grey land crabs that live in the high limestone plateaus, hiding deep in crevices and crannies during the long dry season and emerging at night to graze; they used to be a popular food and young children would compete to see who could catch the most. Land snails are found on all the islands, of all shapes and sizes, hiding away during the long hot summer months but emerging with the arrival of the rain. Until recently the bigger ones were eaten and their shells put to various domestic uses.

There are plenty of pests: the caves and livestock quarters of the mountain areas are infested with fleas, especially bad in the summer monsoon months; bedbugs flourish in dwellings at lower altitudes; the rains bring their usual quota of small biting flies; and a wonderful variety of ticks cause the livestock to itch and scratch. Their misery is often lessened by the Soqotra and Somali starlings who sit on their backs pecking away at anything that moves. The many termites can be a nuisance when they start eating house beams, and the soldier termites can give a nasty nip, but are otherwise harmless. The only truly unpleasant flying insect is an innocent-looking fly called locally *Di Azer*; it favours shady areas under trees in the hot weather and ejects a blob of spittle which contains tiny larvae. These can cause great irritation if they get in the eye, and if swallowed cause an unpleasant, long-lasting cough. However, their preferred victims are sheep and goats, and the islanders say that if you keep your mouth shut, or cover your face with a corner of your headcloth when passing through such areas you will be all right!

Soqotra's isolation has been as potent a factor in its history as in its flora and fauna. Archaeological and historical records are still too limited to interfere with the sense of continuity with the past, as one sees in the timeless occupations of Soqotrans, their dependence on and use of the archipelago's resources only recently changed by better communications with the mainland. Archaeological research is almost as cloud-covered as the mountains: mile upon mile of 'walls' of rough boulders, a flint tool workshop, tombs covered with massive stone slabs – they all need more clarification. Medieval mention of the islands – Alexander settling Greeks there, the conversions to Christianity and Islam, stories of pirates and sorcerers – is still part of legend and hearsay.

From the latter half of the fifteenth century Soqotra was under the control of the Mahrah

Bani Afrar from the mainland, under the Sultan of Qishn. It was a Mahri pilot, Ibn Majid, who guided Portuguese interlopers in the Indian Ocean from Malindi to India in 1498. In 1507 they planted a military colony near the ancient commercial settlement of Suq from which it was hoped they would control those Indian Ocean trade routes. Climate, disease and a generally hostile population soon made Aden and the Red Sea a more attractive (but equally unsuccessful) option. And British schemes to establish a coaling station there in the nineteenth century were also scuppered by monsoon and malaria and the reluctance of the Sultan to sell the island anyway. The Mahrah continued to control the island until the late 1960s but allowed the British to build a landing ground for the RAF during World War II. It was considered part of Eastern Aden Protectorate until 1967 when the Sultanate of Mahra and Socotra was finally abolished; the last ruler's modest palace can still be seen in Hadiboh. Soqotra became part of the PDRY and since 1990 has been part of a unified Yemen.

Today the people of coastal communities such as the main settlements of Qalansiyah, Qadheb and Hadiboh typify the Indian Ocean crossroads, open to its cultural infusions. They include Hadhramis from the Hadhramawt as well as from East Africa and a scattering of Arabs from elsewhere. There are also descendants of the former slave population or of shipwrecked or deserting seamen. Inhabitants of the interior are less diffuse. Serjeant in the 1950s described them as 'separate and secretive, and except for a few of the menfolk who trade in the town (they) have no other contacts. They are shy of strangers and when strangers are visiting warning cries are given, which repeated, echo across the valleys ahead to allow time for the womenfolk to hide from visitors.'[137]

Waterfront at Qalansiyah, the second market town on Soqotra after the capital Hadiboh

Today they are no longer so isolated; inevitably the construction of an airfield has meant the regular to-ing and fro-ing of inhabitants as well as the arrival of outsiders with alluring merchandise.

Nevertheless Soqotrans have a way of life, a language (Soqotri, a pre-literate language which is one of a group of six called the Modern South Arabian languages, to distinguish them from the epigraphic South Arabian of the ancient kingdoms of Yemen), a rich tradition of poetry and songs that are distinct from the mainland, reflecting a pastoral and remarkably peaceful life: in contrast to the fiercely armed tribesmen of the mainland Soqotrans are praised for their skills in defusing argument and tension before it flares into anger and children are brought up to become adroit at diverting potential combatants.

The care of their livestock dominates the lives of most people. They may own and live for some of the year in houses but they also practise transhumance, moving seasonally with their herds between higher and lower pastures of the highland plateau, where they will often live in caves. They raise cattle, sheep, goats and to a lesser extent camels and donkeys, the two latter primarily as baggage animals, crucial in a land with virtually no interior roads. Livestock, mainly goats, have always been raised primarily for milk, made into butter which is clarified as butter oil or ghee. Carefully made and well stored, this keeps almost indefinitely – it used to be the only item reliably in demand from the trading boats which visited the islands, and which they could use as barter for those necessities they could not produce themselves – material for clothing, cereals, dates for the many who had no access to date gardens, and other items such as fishing equipment, iron for knives and other implements. As for the slaughtered animal, every scrap is used – meat, skins, horns, wool.

Transhumance is determined by the availability of grazing, browsing and above all water, supremely important to this pastoral society and symbolised, as on the mainland, by well-made cisterns, reservoirs and channels of indeterminate 'ancient' date. In the high Haggeher mountains water is seldom far away and the long season of drizzle, heavy cloud and rain means that houses here even have gutters, often made from hollow branches of the dragon's blood tree. Even in the dry watercourses of the valleys leading down from this central mountainous area wells can usually be dug. In other parts of the island, rare small springs occur, usually at the base of limestone cliffs. But on the more accessible areas of the plateau rain tends often to be sporadic, seldom covering the whole island; grazing areas are precisely organised according to clan or tribal claims and in times of drought are carefully shared with others. The owner of the land gives his visitors areas which they may make use of until their own rangeland has recovered: the sheep are allotted an area in the upland plains, the cattle in the low-lying land in the valleys, the goats a given area of brushwood.

Just as coastal people depend on livestock in the monsoon season when fishing is impossible, so many pastoralists are seasonal fishermen: when the date harvest is over and before the winter rains fall and the rangeland is once again green, they fish from the shore with line and hook, or cast small-meshed nets in the shallows. Others set fish traps or stun fish in the lagoons and in the water around the mangroves by throwing latex or the crushed tips of various plants into the water. Occasionally they catch one of the many turtles who come ashore to lay their eggs, and all kinds of shellfish as well as sea slugs can be gathered at low tide. The gill flaps (*operculae*) of the largest species of shellfish are sold to the mainland for use in incense mixtures.

Fish were caught for local consumption only, until mainland markets became open to the islanders. Now that fibreglass skiffs powered by outboard motors have replaced the old wooden canoes caulked with shark-liver oil, artisanal fishing has become an important subsistence activity for the people of Soqotra, Abd al-Kuri and Samha (reportedly contributing as much as seventy per cent of the of the islands' economic activity). The islanders of Samha and Abd al-Kuri now rely entirely on fishing as a means of livelihood, their goats and sheep now mostly turned loose to fend for themselves, being brought to the villages only when in milk.

In areas in the interior where adequate water supplies permit the cultivation of date palms, village communities of a more settled type have become established. Even there the inhabitants also own livestock and maintain close relationships with the more pastoralist communities around them, whose members anyway frequently share date plantations with them, and to whom they are often related by marriage. In such better-watered areas the tiny fields and seed beds where the finger millet used to be grown are still visible, though most of them have now been turned over to the growing of dates. The valleys behind the

Islanders carry a Ziziphus spina-christi *tree trunk for house building, much valued because of its resistance to termites*

Haggeher mountains also have great numbers of the precious *Ziziphus spina-christi* tree: precious because not only do they provide food for both humans and animals, but also the best termite-resistant building wood of the island. Their leaves have many medicinal uses as well as being used to wash the hair and prepare the dead for burial. The Ziziphus trees are carefully managed here, being pruned regularly while the young saplings are trained to grow tall and straight with a single trunk.

Overlaid on this pattern of coastal villages, pastoral homesteads and more or less settled date-growing villages is the division of the island into east and west. The western half of the island, from Terr Ditrur in the centre to the furthest west of the island, is markedly different from the eastern half. Lack of water has made all cultivation impossible. It has very few trees, and many of the older habitations were actually built underground, partly to keep cool but also because there was so little wood for building. It is entirely without date cultivation (other than the date gardens around the western capital of Qalansiyah and Qeysoh) and also entirely without cattle, donkeys (indeed they arouse great revulsion) and camels.

There are not many local crafts but, as on the mainland, women weave date-palm fibre into a variety of mats, bags, food containers and so on, and work skins and hides into skins for water, milk and dates. Soqotran women also spin sheeps' wool and on ground looms weave narrow strips which are then sewn together to make attractive rugs, sometimes with cotton woven into them as decoration; Soqotran sheeps' wool rugs were exported to the Yemen over a thousand years ago, for they are mentioned by the Yemeni historian al Hamdani. The islanders commonly plant cotton trees which are carefully protected from livestock with thorny fences in order to produce cotton for their rugs, though the dyes have to be imported. They also use the cotton for laying out the dead and for making little pads which they soak in perfumed oils and tuck inside their ears before going to a party. Women also work clay by hand into various cooking and water pots and incense burners: the water pots and incense burners are arrestingly decorated with the vivid crimson dragon's blood.

The archipelago began to be opened up to the outside world under the PDRY. The first schools were opened, water resources developed, vehicle tracks laboriously constructed (by hand in the early years) into the interior, and medical services and postal services introduced. Small fibreglass fishing boats replaced the dug-out canoes and new markets for fish were found. Food supplies were stockpiled for the monsoon months and distributed throughout the islands; building materials were subsidised and even the inhabitants of the interior began to build houses. Although some in the poorer, western end of the island remember a time without money and then recall the arrival of the silver 'rupee' and rare silver Maria Theresa thaler, the old system of barter easily gave way to the cash economy of the new government.

Soqotra poses a challenge for the government of Yemen which seeks to develop the island, improve the hard lives of the people and also preserve this unique environment. By far the biggest change since unification has been the opening of an all-weather airstrip in 1998. At last there can be regular flights to and from the island the year round, including during the monsoon months. In 1996 the Yemeni Government ratified the International Convention on Biodiversity and in the same year declared the Soqotra Archipelago a special, natural area in urgent need of protection.

The winter rainy season: view from the Haggeher mountains to a well-watered valley, where villagers cultivate extensive date gardens

In 1997 the Global Environment Facility agreed to fund a five-year project 'Conservation and Sustainable Use of the Biodiversity of the Soqotra Archipelago' and in 2000 the government approved its proposal for a zoning plan. This aims to ensure that the much-needed development of the islands proceeds in a carefully planned manner in sympathy with the unique environment and character of the archipelago.

Already the widely dispersed one- or two-family settlements of earlier years have begun to cluster together, close to available services such as access tracks and new water facilities. The European Union has been asked to prepare a ten-year plan for social and economic development of the archipelago, and there is much talk of improved fishing facilities, ice plants, water development, new roads, development of the livestock sector and new agricultural enterprises. Especially there is talk about

a possible future for the island as an eco-tourist destination whereby visitors would learn something of the culture and way of life of these very special islands. By observing the islanders making pottery, palm and rug weaving, cultivating their dates or building their unusual houses and seeing how they conserve water and manage their livestock, visitors come to appreciate how man in this small group of islands managed so successfully to live in harmony with his environment and with his fellow men and women.

The final word might go to the Bents, who were clearly deeply moved by their short stay on the island of Soqotra: 'It was pleasant to be among such friendly people, who had no horror of us and did not even seem much surprised at seeing us there, and to be able to go off quite alone for a scramble so safely … A more peaceful, law-abiding people it would be hard to find elsewhere.'[138]

XI POSTSCRIPT – YEMEN TODAY

'The nature and local circumstances of [this part of] Arabia are favourable to the spirit of independence,' wrote Carsten Niebuhr, ' which distinguishes its inhabitants from other nations. Their deserts and mountains have always secured them from the encroachments of conquest.' And in a sense he was almost right. When looking at Yemen's history, especially in the truncated form presented here, two aspects stand out: the physical and political turbulence of its highland core, remote and often untouched by the wider world; but also the force of the ocean washing its shores, pulling it willy-nilly into that wider world.

The 1970s and 1980s saw a constant tug-of-war between northern and southern Yemen. Divided by the Cold War, they were unable to make the concessions necessary to erase the illogical frontier that had been imposed between them. Meanwhile the country's strategic position, guarding the Red Sea, thrust it into the forefront of Cold War planning, somewhat to the advantage of both north and south: every ally wanted to build roads, develop harbours, set up fish freezers and cotton factories. Even the waterless rock of Perim was once more occupied, this time by the Russians, no doubt every bit as reluctantly as John Avery's pirate companions or the telegraph operators of Britain's imperial cable network.

The end of the Cold War undoubtedly facilitated Yemen's unification in 1990, neither east nor west needing any longer to bolster the fortunes of little allies. The withdrawal of Soviet and other communist aid from the south made union with the north essential, a shot-gun wedding which everyone had debated for years but for the speedy achievement of which no one was quite prepared. The speed could have been the undoing of the new Republic of Yemen, the 1990s taken up with painful and unsatisfactory bargaining among the various pressure groups within the country – tribal, regional, religious – particularly in 1994. But it has survived, the achievement all the more remarkable when the dire economic impact of Yemen's neutrality over the 1991 Gulf War is taken into account.

Yemen is a land of bitter-sweet contrasts: the violence of so much of the landscape countered by a pool of water, a field of ripening sorghum, the setting sun irradiating façades of a mud village, a sudden gesture of hospitality. The geological upheavals of the Rift Valley with which we began this story, the hands stretched across the Red Sea between Africa and Asia, the pull of the Indian Ocean, the continuity of culture form a unique microcosm. We come as sojourners, humbled by the beauty and antiquity, returning enriched to our whirling worlds, tempted always to return.

Opposite: *View south-east along the new mountain road to the Lawdar plain*

Village perched on the spur of a hill in the highlands north of Ta'izz

CHRONOLOGY

BC

Palaeolithic remains
5th–4th mill	Earliest settlements
3rd–2nd mill	Bronze Age: signs of religious cults
2nd mill	Domestication of camel
1st mill	Emergence of city states, Saba, Ma'in, Qataban, Hadhramawt, Awsan
c.800	Earliest inscriptions
6th–5th c	Marib temples and dam
c.2nd c	Rise of Himyarites
24	Aelius Gallus' Arabian expedition

AD

1st–3rd c	Political and economic shift to central highlands
1st c	*Periplus of the Erythraean Sea*
2nd c	Roman development of sea route to India
3rd–4th c	Judaism and Christianity established
c.520	Marib dam burst, scattering Qahtan tribes over southern Arabia
523	Massacre of Najran Christians by Jewish ruler Dhu Nawas
525	Ethiopians occupy Yemen; Himyarite state collapses
575	Ethiopians replaced with Persian occupation
c.570	Birth of Prophet Muhammad
622	Prophet's flight to Madina; start of Muslim *hijrah* calendar
630s	Yemen's conversion to Islam begins; establishment of Islamic caliphate. Centralised rule by 'Umayyads (Damascus) & 'Abbasids (Baghdad)
9th c	Yu'firid dynasty in central highlands
819–1018	Ziyadid dynasty in Tihamah
844	Ahmad ibn Isa al-Muhajir arrives in Hadhramawt

890s	Al-Hadi ila l-Haqq establishes Zaydi Imamate
1047–1138	Isma'ili Sulayhid dynasty
1173–1228	Ayyubid dynasty
1228–1454	Rasulid dynasty
late 14th c	Coffee-drinking al-Shadhili arrives in Mokha from Ethiopia
1454–1517	Tahirid dynasty
1504	First Portuguese vessel in Red Sea
1517	Mamluk invasion; Mamluk defeat in Egypt by Ottoman Turks
1539–mid-17th c	First Ottoman occupation of Yemen
16th c	Kathiris in Hadhramawt invite Yafa'i mercenaries to help them
1763	Danish expedition, including Carsten Niebuhr
1798	Napoleon's Egyptian expedition
1839	British capture Aden
1869	Inauguration of Suez Canal
1872–1918	Second Ottoman occupation of northern Yemen
1904–1948	Imam Yahya expels Ottomans, rules northern Yemen
1934	Anglo-Yemeni treaty establishes *de facto* frontier between north and south
1937	Aden becomes British colony
1948	Imam Yahya assassinated, succeeded by son Ahmad
1962	Federal constitution established in south
1962–70	Republic declared, Imamate abolished; civil war in northern Yemen; establishment of Yemen Arab Republic (YAR)
1967	Independence in southern Yemen; establishment of People's Democratic Republic of Yemen (PDRY)
1990	Unification of north and south; establishment of Republic of Yemen
1994	Suppression of southern uprising

GLOSSARY

abaya	black covering garment worn by city women
angarib	string bed of Tihamah
bara'	dance
barakah	blessing, blessedness
bunn	coffee bean
diwan	sitting or reception room
faqih	wise, benevolent
futah	skirt cloth worn like sarong
ghayl	water channel, often underground
hajj	pilgrimage to Mecca, an obligation for Muslims
haram	sacred area, as in *haram* of Mecca
hawtah	sacred area, used in Hadhramawt
hijrah	neutral territory; but also flight, as used to mark Islamic calendar
hilbah	fenugreek, used for green sauce on *saltah*
'imamah	silver and gold embroidered turban wound round cap (*qawiq*) worn by *sayyids* and *qadhis*
janbiyyah	dagger
kidam	small round loaves of flour and ground lentils
lahuh	pancake type bread similar to Ethiopian *injera*
madrasah	religious school
mafraj	sitting room, sometimes at top of house
maghmuk	tie-dyed cotton face mask worn by San'ani women
mamluk	owned, hence slave, esp. of soldiers
mihrab	niche identifying *qiblah* wall giving direction to Mecca
miqshamah	vegetable garden in San'a old city
musnad	term for South Arabian scripts
qabili	tribesman
qadhi	judge
qahwah	coffee drink
qat	*Catha edulis*, chewed by Yemenis
qiblah	wall in prayer hall of mosque giving direction to Mecca
qishr	husk of coffee bean, as a drink infused with spices
qudad	lime plaster used for waterproofing roofs, cisterns etc
qushmi	horse radish, white radish grown in San'ani vegetable gardens
rayhan	basil
sabil	source of drinking water provided by devout Muslims
saltah	meat and vegetable stew served for lunch with *hilbah*
samsarah	warehouse or caravanserai near market area
sayil	flood water
sayyid	descendant of the Prophet, member of religious aristocracy
shari'ah	Islamic law derived from the Quran and other sources
siqayah	source of drinking water provided by devout Muslims in south
sitarah	'tablecloth'-like garment worn particularly by San'ani women
sufi	Muslim mystic
suq	market
thumma	dagger
'urf	customary law, complementing Quranic law (*shari'ah*)
'ushshah	palm and sorghum straw dwelling in Tihamah
wadi	natural water channel, valley or gorge
wali	holy man
zabib	raisins
zabur	building method using layers of mud mixed with chopped straw
ziyarah	usually visit, used for visit to tomb of *wali*

NOTES

Full details of the books and articles referred to will be found in the Suggested Further Reading p. 154

Chapter I

1   Rihani 1
2   See A. Thompson, *The Origins of Arabia* (London 2000) for an overview of Arabian geology
3   N. N. Ambraseys, C. D. Melville, R. D. Adams, in *Seismicity of Egypt and the Red Sea* (Cambridge 1994), have recorded all earth movements in the area between 184 BC and 1992 AD
4   Varanda 44-46
5   Belhaven 201
6   Ibn Battuta/Gibb 109
7   C. J. Cruttenden, 'A journey from Mocha to Sanaa', *Geographical Journal* 1838/8 267; on the ibex hunt see R. B. Serjeant, *The South Arabian Hunt* (London 1976)
8   Mackintosh-Smith 16-28. Other authorities on qat are Shelagh Weir, Kevin Rushby and John G. Kennedy
9   Belhaven 112
10   Varanda 116-17

Chapter II

11   For an overview of current scholarship, see catalogues of Paris and Munich exhibitions; also *AAE* 1995, a memorial issue for A. F. L. Beeston
12   Now the General Organisation for Antiquities and Manuscripts (GOAM)
13   N. M. Whalen & K. E. Schatte, 'Pleistocene sites in southern Yemen', *AAE* 1997 1-10
14   H. A. McClure, 'A new Arabian Stone Age assemblage', *AAE* 1994 1-16; H. Amirkhanov on Palaeolithic and Neolithic sites in the same volume, 217-28
15   A. de Maigret, *The Bronze Age Culture of Khawlan al-Tiyal* (Rome IsMEO 1990)
16   J. F. Breton, 'Wadi Surban', *PSAS* 2000 49-61
17   T. J. Wilkinson, C. Edens, M. Gibson, 'The archaeology of the Yemen high plains: a preliminary chronology', *AAE* 1997 99-142; also *AAE* 1999 1-34
18   B. Vogt & A. Sedov, 'The Sabir culture and coastal Yemen during the 2nd millennium BCE', *PSAS* 1998 261-70
19   N. Groom's *Frankincense and Myrrh* is the best overview of this pre-Islamic incense world
20   See K. Kitchen, *Documentation* II for an update on the chronology issue
21   Pliny the Elder, *Natural History* Bk VI ch 32 for a description of contemporary Arabia
22   For the earlier excavations see R. L. Bowen & F. P. Albright 1958. Their work is being continued by the American Foundation for the Study of Man: see W. Glanzman, 'Digging deeper', *PSAS* 1998 89-104
23   See C. Robin, 'A propos des inscriptions *in situ* de Baraqish', *PSAS* 1979 102-12
24   A. de Maigret & C. Robin, *Le temple de Nakrah à Baraqish* (Paris 1993)
25   Bowen & Albright *op.cit.*
26   Groom 171
27   See A. Sedov, 'New archaeological and epigraphic material from Qana', *AAE* 1992 110-37
28   Belhaven 9
29   H. St John Philby, *Sheba's Daughters* 85-99
30   See J. F. Breton, 'Shabwa, capitale antique du Hadhramawt', *Journal Asiatique* 1987/1-2 13-34
31   See W. Glanzman's articles in *PSAS* 1998, 1999, 2001
32   Doe *Monuments* 205
33   See F. D. P. Wicker, 'The road to Punt', *Geographical Journal* 1998 155-67; also K. Kitchen, 'Further thoughts on Punt and its neighbours', *Studies on Ancient Egypt* (London 1999)
34   Pliny, *Natural History* Bk 12 ch 32, quoted Groom 136-7
35   A. Sedov, 'New archaeological and epigraphic material from Qana', *AAE* 1992 110-38
36   Wellsted II 421-24
37   A good overview of early Arabian languages and scripts is by M. C. A. Macdonald,

'Reflections on the linguistic map of pre-Islamic Arabia', *AAE* 2000 28-79; see also the great master of South Arabian epigraphy, the late A. F. L. Beeston whose numerous books, articles and reviews are listed in Macdonald, 'Bibliography' 1997; also 'In memoriam Beeston', ed. F. Stone *Arabian Studies* 1995

38 Groom, 'The Roman expedition into South Arabia', *Bulletin for Society for Arabian Studies* 1996 5-8, 23

Chapter III

39 A. F. L.Beeston, 'New light on the Himyarite calendar', *Arabian Studies* I 1974 1-6
40 al-Hamdani/Faris 40
41 See *Jemen* 386-87 (catalogue nos 456, 457)
42 Serjeant & Lewcock 44-48
43 Mackintosh-Smith 9
44 Serjeant & Lewcock 44
45 Cruttenden 245
46 Niebuhr I 340
47 See Lewcock 1986

Chapter IV

48 By far the best description of the city, yesterday and today, is Serjeant & Lewcock's *San'a*
49 See T. Marchand, 'Reconsidering the role of the mosque minaret in San'a' *PSAS* 1999 95-101
50 See Varanda 265-291 on architecture and building techniques in San'a
51 Jourdain 93
52 Cruttenden 245
53 Niebuhr I 340, II 75
54 Niebuhr I 407
55 See C. Smith, 'Kawkaban: some of its history', *Arabian Studies* VI 1992 35-50

Chapter V

56 Varanda 108-09
57 L. & J. Greenough, 'Iron Age gold mining: a preliminary report on camps in the al-Maraziq region, Yemen', *AAE* 2000 223-36
58 For more discussion of Yemen's religious history see Stookey 79-94
59 On the *Ahrar*, see J. Leigh Douglas, *The Free Yemeni Movement 1935-62* (Beirut 1987); also Claudie Fayein, *A French Doctor in the Yemen* (London 1958)

60 See P. Dresch on Yemeni tribalism *in Tribes, Government & History in Yemen* (Oxford 1989)
61 Translation by Ibrahim al-Kibsi
62 Niebuhr II 350
63 Quoted in Serjeant & Lewcock 80
64 J. Halévy, 'Mission archéologique dans le Yemen', *Journal Asiatique* XIX 1872 5-98
65 See Wyman Bury, *Arabia Infelix*, for the second Ottoman occupation
66 On the history of Jews in Yemen, see T. Parfitt, *The Road to Redemption: the Jews of Yemen 1900-50* (Leiden 1996)
67 See R. Wilson, 'Regular and permanent markets in the San'a region', *Arabian Studies* IV 1978 189-92
68 See Ahmad al-Shani, 'Yemeni literature in Hajjah prisons', *Arabian Studies* II 1975 43-60
69 See R. Porter, S. Christensen, P. Schiermacker-Hansen, *Field Guide to the Birds of the Middle East* (London 1996)

Chapter VI

70 See C. Phillips, 'The Tihamah *c.*5000 BCE-500 BCE', *PSAS* 1998 233-70
71 Niebuhr I 247
72 Smith, 'Studies on the Tihamah', *JRAS* 1986/I in a review of F. Stone's book of the same title
73 D. Varisco, in *Medieval Agriculture & Islamic Science: the almanac of a Yemeni Sultan* (Seattle 1994) is a leading authority
74 As well as Stone's *Tihamah* see Varanda 132-55
75 For articles on historical Zabid see E. Keall in *PSAS* 1983 53-69; 1984 51-65; 1999 79-96
76 Ibn Battuta/Gibb 108
77 See Stone 1985 120-24
78 Smith, *Miscellany* 135
79 *Periplus*/Casson 63
80 J. Baldry, 'Foreign interventions and occupations of Kamaran Island', *Arabian Studies* IV 1978 89-112
81 'It is not for me to criticise an undertaking that lacked neither zeal nor ability,' wrote G. Wyman Bury of the railway project in *Arabia Infelix*, but he did so in no uncertain terms (126-29)
82 For its earlier history see Baldry, 'The early history of the Yemeni port of al-Hudaydah', *Arabian Studies* VII 1985 37-52

83   Jourdain 103
84   Middleton's travails are described in J. de la
      Roque, *Voyage*, 250-287, (London 1732)
85   See Searight 1980, 37
86   See P. Boxall, 'Diary of a coffee agent',
      Arabian Studies I 1974 102-118; and C. G.
      Brouwer, *The Dutch East India Company
      in Yemen 1614-55* (Amsterdam 1997)

Chapter VII
87   Jourdain 84
88   For more on the Isma'ilis and Bohras see
      Stookey 49-78
89   al-Hakami/Kay 21-47
90   Jourdain 84
91   See Smith, 1978, for the history of this period
92   Ibn Battuta/Gibb 109
93   al-Khazraji, quoted by Smith, 'The Yemenite
      settlement of Tha'bat: historical,
      numismatic and epigraphic notes',
      Arabian Studies I 119-34
94   de Varthema 35
95   See David Holden, *Farewell to Arabia* (London
      1966) 69-87 for the last years of the Imamate
96   C. Myntti, 'Notes on mystical healers in the
      Hujuriyyah', *Arabian Studies* VIII/1990
      171-76
97   See Smith, 'The Tahirid Sultans of the Yemen
      858-923/1454-1517, and their historian
      Ibn al-Daybi', *Journal of Semitic Studies*
      29/1984 141-54
98   de Varthema 44
99   Selma al-Radi: see bibliography
100   See Serjeant 1963 for Arab views on the
      Portuguese incursions into the Red Sea

Chapter VIII
101   J. T. & M. Bent 86
102   Stark 87
103   There are numerous articles in *AAE* on the
      archaeology of southern Yemen, see in
      particular A. Hizri, 'Research on
      Palaeolithic & Neolithic sites of
      Hadhramaut & Mahra' *AAE* 1996/5 217-28;
      also A. Sedov, 'Notes on an archaeological
      map of the Hadhramawt', *AAE* 1996/7
104   H. Ingrams 140
105   The most penetrating study of the social and
      economic scene in Hadhramawt is by Harold
      Ingrams' wife Doreen: see bibliography

106   See Serjeant, *The Sayyids of Hadramawt*
      (London 1957)
107   See Damluji, 1993
108   Lewcock, *Shibam*
109   Stark 218
110   H. Ingrams 191
111   For the early history of al-Shihr, see
      C. Hardy-Guibert, 'Archaeological
      research at al-Shihr', *PSAS* 2001 69-80
112   Wellsted was on the original survey voyage
      when he spotted the Himyarite inscription
      on Husn al-Ghurab west of Mukalla
113   *Periplus*/Casson 165
114   H. Ingrams 233
115   H. Ingrams 223
116   Allfree 97 ff
117   Stark 227

Chapter IX
118   Serjeant, 1963, translates some of the Arab
      reactions to these incursions
119   Waugh, *A Tourist in Africa* 36
120   *Periplus*/Casson 65
121   Marco Polo, *Travels*, (Everyman edition) 401-02
122   Duarte Barbosa 54
123   Albuquerque's version of his attack on Aden is
      in his *Commentaries* Bk IV (Hakluyt series
      59/1884)
124   de Varthema 26
125   Valentia II 1809
126   Bombay, *Asiatic Journal* NS XIV 1834
127   Wellsted I 424
128   For development of steam communications
      through the Red Sea, see Searight, 1991
129   Harris, *Journey* 123
130   Wyman Bury *Arabia Infelix*
131   Scott, *High Yemen* 69
132   Stookey 189, quoting Nazih al-Azm who
      visited Yemen as an interpreter for the
      American engineer Karl Twitchell
133   Fred Halliday, in *Arabia without Sultans*,
      describes well this period of confrontation
      between north and south

Chapter X
134   Serjeant, in Doe 135
135   Bent 379-80
136   *ibid* 389
137   Serjeant/Doe 31
138   Bent 393

SUGGESTED FURTHER READING

Throughout its history Yemen has attracted a great many historians. The list below contains the bare bones of those I consider most useful in sustaining and expanding a knowledge of Yemen. Many of them include extensive bibliographies for yet further enquiry. Articles mentioned in the footnotes are not included, but will be found in the following periodicals:

Arabian Archaeology and Epigraphy (AAE)
Arabian Studies
Bulletin of the Society for Arabian Studies
Journal Asiatique
Journal of the Royal Asiatic Society (JRAS)
Proceedings of the Seminar for Arabian Studies (PSAS)

All of these include articles by the great scholars of Yemen, many of them referred to in the endnotes.

The Encyclopaedia of Islam New Series (EI²) is also an invaluable source

Allfree, P. S., *Hawks of the Hadhramawt*, London 1967
al-'Amri, Husayn ibn 'Abd Allah, *The Yemen in the Eighteenth and Nineteenth Centuries*, London 1985
Auchterlonie, Paul, *Yemen. World Bibliographical Series* vol. 50, London, Clio Press 1998
Balfour-Paul, Jenny, *Indigo in the Arab World*, Richmond, Surrey 1997
Barbosa, Duarte, *A Description of the Coasts of East Africa and Malabar in the Beginning of the 16th century*, trs H. E. J. Stanley London 1866
Belhaven, Master of (R.A. Hamilton), *The Kingdom of Melchior*, London 1949
Bent, J. T. and Mrs, *Southern Arabia*, London 1900
Bidwell, Robin, *The Two Yemens*, London 1983
Travellers in Arabia, London 1976
Bowen R. L. and Albright F. P. (eds), *Archaeological Discoveries in South Arabia*, Baltimore 1958
Bowersock, G. W., *Roman Arabia*, London 1983
Breton, J. F., *L'Arabie heureuse au temps de la reine de Saba*, Paris n.d.
Fouilles de Shabwa, Paris 1992
Burrowes, Robert D., *The historical dictionary of Yemen*, Lanham Md 1995
Bury, G.W., *Arabia Infelix*, London 1915
The Land of Uz, London 1911
Casson, Lionel (trs), *The Periplus Maris Erythraei*, Princeton 1989
Chelhod, Joseph, *L'Arabie du Sud: histoire et civilisation*, 3 vols, Paris 1985
Costa, Paolo & E. Vicario, *Arabia Felix: a land of builders*, New York 1977
Damluji, Selma Samar, *The Valley of Mud-brick Architecture*, London 1993
Daum, Werner (ed), *Yemen: 3,000 Years of Art & Civilisation*, Innsbruck 1987
Doe, Brian, *Monuments of Arabia*, Cambridge 1983
Southern Arabia, London 1971
Socotra, Island of Tranquillity, with contributions by R. B. Serjeant, A. Radcliffe Smith and K. M. Guichard, London 1992
Dresch, Paul, *A History of Modern Yemen*, (Cambridge, Cambridge University Press, 2000)
Finster, Barbara, 'An outline of the history of Islamic religious architecture in Yemen', *Muqarnas* 9/1992 124-46
Freitag, Ulrike, and Clarence-Smith, W., *Hadhrami Traders and Statesmen in the Indian Ocean* 1750-1960s Leiden 1997
Glaser, Eduard, *Altjemenische Nachtrichten*, Munich 1906
Groom, Nigel, *Frankincense & Myrrh: a study of the Arabian incense trade*, London 1981
al-Hakami, 'Umarah ibn 'Ali, *Yaman, Its Early Medieval History*, trs by H. C. Kay, London 1892
Halliday, Fred, *Arabia without Sultans*, New York 1985
al-Hamdani, Abu Muhammad al-Hasan, *Kitab al-iklil*, trs as *Antiquities of Southern Arabia* by N.A. Faris, 1938
Hansen, Thorkild, *Arabia Felix*, London 1964
Harris, Walter, *Journey through the Yemen*, London 1893
Ibn Battuta, Muhammad ibn 'Abd Allah, *Travels in Asia and Africa*, trs H. A. R. Gibb, London 1983
Ingrams, Doreen, *A survey of the social and economic conditions in the Aden Protectorate*, Asmara 1949

Ingrams, Harold, *Arabia and the Isles*, London 1942

Jemen: Kunst und Archäologie im Land der Königin von Saba', Vienna 1998 (catalogue of Yemen exhibition in Vienna 1998-99)

Jourdain, John, *Journals 1608-17*, Hakluyt Society second series vol. 16, London 1905

Kennedy John G., *Eating the Flower of Paradise*, Dordrecht 1987

al-Khazraji, 'Ali ibn al-Hasan, *The Pearl Strings: a history of the Resuliyy dynasty of Yemen*, trs. J.W. Redhouse, Leiden-London 1906-18

Kitchen, Kenneth, *Documentation for Ancient Arabia*, Liverpool: Part I, 1994; Part II, 2000

Lewcock, Ronald, *The Old Walled City of San'a*, UNESCO 1986

Wadi Hadhramaut & the Walled City of Shibam, Paris 1986

Macdonald, M. C. A., 'A bibliography of A. F .L. Beeston', *PSAS* 27, 1997 21-48

Mackintosh-Smith, Tim, *Yemen: Travels in Dictionary Land*, London 1997

Macro, Eric, *Yemen and the Western World since 1571*, London 1968

Maigret, Alessandro de, *Arabia felix: un viaggio nell'archeologia dello Yemen*, Milan 1996 (English edition, London 2002)

The Bronze Age Culture of Khawlan al-Tiyal and al-Hada, Rome 1990

Marco Polo, *Travels,* Everyman edition, London 1936

Mountnorris, George Annesley (Lord Valentia), *Voyages & Travels in India etc*, 3 vols, London 1808-09

Niebuhr, Carsten, *Voyage en Arabie & en autres pays circonvoisins*, 2 vols, Amsterdam and Utrecht, 1776 (in English, Edinburgh 1792)

Philby, H. St. J., *Sheba's Daughters*, London 1939

Phillips, Wendell, *Qataban & Sheba*, New York/London 1955

al-Radi, Selma, *The 'Amiriya in Rada'* (Oxford series in Islamic art XIII), Oxford 1997

Rihani, Ameen, *Arabian Peak & Desert*, London 1930

de la Roque, J, *Voyage to Arabia Felix*, London 1732

Scott, Hugh, *In the High Yemen*, London 1942

Searight, Sarah, *The British in the Middle East*, London 1981

Steaming East, London 1991

Serjeant R. B., *The Portuguese off the South Arabian Coast*, Beirut 1974

Serjeant, R. B. & Lewcock, Ronald (eds), *San'a: an Arabian Islamic city*, London 1983

Smith G. Rex, *The Ayyubids and early Rasulids in Yemen*, London 1978

Arabian and Islamic Studies, Harlow 1983 (ed. with A. K. Irvine, R. B. Serjeant, *A Miscellany of Middle East Articles: in memoriam Thomas Muir Johnstone*, Harlow 1988,

'The Yemenite settlement of the Tha'bat: historical, numismatic & epigraphic notes', *Arabian Studies* VI, Cambridge, 1982

Studies in the Medieval History of Yemen and South Arabia, Aldershot 1997

Stark, Freya, *The Southern Gates of Arabia*, London 1936

Stone, Francine (ed), *Studies on the Tihama*, London 1985

Stookey, Robert, *Yemen: the politics of the Yemen Arab Republic*, Boulder, Colorado 1978

Varanda, Fernando, *The Art of Building in Yemen*, London 1981

de Varthema, Ludovico, *Travels*, ed & introd by G. P. Badger, London 1863

Weir, Sheila, *Qat in Yemen*, London 1985

Wellsted, J. R., *Travels in Arabia*, 2 vols, London 1838

Yemen au pays de la reine de Saba, Institut du Monde Arabe: catalogue of exhibition, Paris, 1997

INDEX

Page numerals in roman refer to a text entry; page numerals in **bold** refer to an illustration.

Yemen
Land and People

Text © Sarah Searight
Soqotra text © Miranda Morris
All photographs © Jane Taylor, except the following:
Admiralty Handbook, *Western Arabia and the Red Sea*, London 1946: p. 123
John Ducker: p. 118; Murray Graham Collection: pp. 125, 130
Merilyn Hywel-Jones Collection: p. 122; Julian Lush: pp. 47, 74, 104, 115, 119
Miranda Morris: pp. 134, 135, 138–9, 140, 143, 145; Venetia Porter: p. 107
Sarah Searight: pp. 16–7, 18, 23 (rt), 24, 25, 43, 48-9, 53, 56, 61, 62, 67, 102, 111, 129
Other illustrations:
Searight Collection, Victoria & Albert Museum: p. 117
J. R. Wellsted, *Travels in Arabia*: p. 40
Carsten Niebuhr, *Voyage en Arabie*: pp. 77, 81, 101
Peninsular & Orient Co.: p. 126

Cover: Shaharah, a Zaydi stronghold in the north of Yemen
Back cover: Traditional and modern in a dried fruit and confectionary shop
in Suq al-Milh, San'a
Half title page: San'a stained glass window

Map by Ted Hammond

Publisher: Alexander Fyjis-Walker
Assistant publisher and editor: Ava Li
Editorial assistant: Barbara Fyjis-Walker
Design editor: James Sutton

Published 2002
by Pallas Athene (Publishers) Ltd

If you would like further information about
Pallas Athene publications,
please write to:
Dept. B, 59 Linden Gardens,
London W2 4HJ
or visit our website:
WWW.PALLASATHENE.CO.UK

ISBN 1 874329 82 7

Printed in Slovenia